SOCIETY AND MEDICINE

NUMBER XVII OF
THE NEW YORK ACADEMY OF MEDICINE
LECTURES TO THE LAITY

SOCIETY AND MEDICINE

LECTURES TO THE LAITY, NO. XVII

THE NEW YORK ACADEMY OF MEDICINE

Iago Galdston, M.D., Editor

Essay Index Reprint Series

BOOKS FOR LIBRARIES PRESS
FREEPORT, NEW YORK

INTERNATIONAL STANDARD BOOK NUMBER:
0-8369-2124-0

LIBRARY OF CONGRESS CATALOG CARD NUMBER:
74-142684

PRINTED IN THE UNITED STATES OF AMERICA

CONTENTS

FOREWORD vii
Howard R. Craig, M.D.
Director, The New York Academy of Medicine

INTRODUCTION ix
Iago Galdston, M.D.

DISEASE AND ITS LOCAL SETTING 3
Sir James Spence, M.D.
Professor of Child Health, Newcastle-upon-Tyne, England

THE BIOLOGY OF ETHICS 20
R. W. Gerard, M.D., Ph.D., D.Sc.
Professor of Physiology, University of Chicago

THE NATURAL HISTORY OF NEUROTIC BEHAVIOR 46
Howard S. Liddell, Ph.D.
Professor of Psychobiology, Cornell University

ENVIRONMENT AND HEREDITY 70
Theodore H. Ingalls, M.D.
Associate Professor of Epidemiology, School of Public Health, Harvard University

CHANGING CONCEPTS OF CHILD CARE:
A Historical Review 83
Milton J. E. Senn, M.D.
Sterling Professor of Pediatrics and Psychiatry; Director, Child Study Center, Yale University

ENVIRONMENT IN NUTRITION 104
Russell M. Wilder, M.D.
Director, National Institute of Arthritis and Metabolism Research, United States Public Health Service, Bethesda, Maryland

INDEX 121

FOREWORD

THE NEW YORK Academy of Medicine takes pride in presenting in this volume the seventeenth annual series of its Lectures to the Laity. These lectures represent one of the most important of the Academy's contributions on the broad front of medical education. Perhaps the greater efforts on the part of the Academy are directed specifically at the medical and the para-medical professions through lectures, clinics, panel discussions, publications, radio and television presentations. However, of recent years it has become increasingly evident that the Academy has taken a more active part in public health in terms of the official City agencies, in community affairs generally and in lay education. This series, initiated in 1935, was its first attempt to apprise the lay public by lecture of the current advances in medical progress. At first the lectures were more particularly directed to discussions of specific diseases. More lately they have attempted to show trends in medical and scientific thinking. This change has been influenced at least in part by the increasing knowledge of medical matters by the lay public and by the vast amount of space devoted to medicine and related subjects in lay periodicals and press. What has been and is urgently needed by the laity in orientation and guidance. These lectures are aimed at satisfying these needs.

The Academy owes a debt of gratitude to the lecturers,

each of whom gave freely of himself and of his competence. To Dr. Harold B. Keyes, Chairman of the Committee on Laity Lectures, who presided at each of the lectures, goes the thanks of the Academy for his skillful and effective handling of the meetings. To each of those individuals who introduced the speakers and to the members of the Committee in charge of the lectures, appreciation is heartily due. And finally, as Director of the Academy, I wish to express my own appreciation of the labors of Dr. Iago Galdston and his staff. It has been due to his imagination, his vision and his knowledge of the far-flung reaches of medicine and the related sciences, that these lectures over all these years have remained stimulating, provocative and productive.

HOWARD R. CRAIG, M.D.

INTRODUCTION

SOCIETY AND MEDICINE is a most fitting title for the collection of essays gathered in this book. Their range in subject matter, their divergence in approach both to society and to medicine, their emphasis on the different aspects which society and medicine present to the inquiring intelligence, afford the reader a fine perspective on the intricate interrelations existing and operating between society and medicine. Such a perspective, so clear and so many-faceted an exposition of these intricate interrelationships is not only patently valuable for and of itself, but is also of immense value as a protection against, or antidote to, the easy and fatuous "cash nexus" equation of the relation between society and medicine. Economics is not the ultimate science nor the sovereign remedy for all individual and social evil. Other sciences, other disciplines, serve to illuminate the methods, processes and problems of society and medicine. They suggest ways in which we may effectively come to grips with the problems, change the methods and improve the processes both of medicine and of societal existence.

Individually, the essays herein published were composed as single expositions in given fields of knowledge. They are, in other words, expositional rather than polemical. But they do fall into a neat pattern which embraces the more important components of societal living—as they bear upon, and are affected by, medicine. This patterning, be it confessed, was not entirely a fortunate accident. It was aimed at by the Committee whose responsibility it is to organize the Laity Lectures.

Sir James Spence, who contributed the first essay, dealing with disease and its local setting, is unfortunately no longer with us. He died a short while after his return to England. Fortunately, however, the work which he describes in his essay is being continued by his younger colleagues. Sir James, as the reader will quickly gather from the overtones and indwelling spirit of the essay, was a man of great charm, of deep but never humorless sincerity, of broad sympathies, a hard worker and a very friendly soul, who had grasped and who labored to make clear and appreciable, the subtle and manifold effects which "setting" has upon disease, and vice versa. Prof. Gerard, in his contribution, ably expounds and skillfully defends the thesis that ethics is rooted in biology and can so be derived. Prof. Liddell, in his essay on "The Natural History of Neurotic Behavior" demonstrates the roles of deprivation, conflict and frustration in the engenderment of pathological behavior. The bearing of Prof. Liddell's exposition to Dr. Gerard's essay will not be missed by the reader. Prof. Ingalls' contribution, so provocatively entitled "Environment in Heredity," does not entirely resolve the issue of Nature vs. Nurture, but does go far in demonstrating the extent to which environment can circumscribe, alter, and deflect the realization of hereditary potentials. Prof. Ingalls' studies were, so to say, confined to intrauterine development. Prof. Milton Senn then carries on, treating of the social and medical factors involved in the process and task of growing up. The series is rounded off with Dr. Wilder's essay on nutrition, that branch of the biological science which is certainly the *alpha* of growth, of development, and of well-being, societal no less than individual.

This series is authoritative in quality, informative in substance, provocative and inspiring in effect. The credit is all the contributors': ours, the pleasures of a modest co-worker, and the satisfaction in witnessing tasks well done.

IAGO GALDSTON, M.D.

New York
March, 1955

SOCIETY AND MEDICINE

DISEASE AND ITS LOCAL SETTING

Sir James Spence, M. D.

I AM no historian, but I think that when the history of this period comes to be written that the conquest of disease will be revealed as one of its greatest achievements. Now, I am not suggesting that the conquest has yet been so great that we are within reach of a physical Elysium where there will be no more sickness, where disease will be eliminated, where all that will be left to harm the bodies of men will be the injuries which come from the machinery which they themselves make. It is, I think, fairly safe to predict that the variety and extent of the use of this new machinery will leave us the trauma, the injury, as one of its results. But, by and large, the major pestilences are now under control, those pestilences which used to sweep the face of the earth. And during the past hundred years we have overcome typhoid and typhus, smallpox and syphilis, plague and puerperal fever, diphtheria, dysentery. And that is, indeed, the limitation of my definition when I say we have, to that extent, conquered disease.

But I think it is wise to remember that Nature is a very fickle mistress, and we must not be too confident of her submission nor of her fidelity. She appears always to have tricks up her sleeve, which we mortals cannot very easily foresee. And if I were to continue to use the metaphor of pagan theology, I would say that men are still the playthings of the gods.

We are, I think, more inclined, though, to take this more modest view nowadays than our parents would have been fifty years ago. They were then living in the flood-tide of self-confidence. "A man is master of his fate and captain of his soul." You will remember the philosophy of the day. Our fathers were then elated by the Darwinian theory of evolution, and they were, perhaps, misreading the theory of evolution into a belief that all change, through physical adaptation, was necessarily progress.

Now, indeed, we are much less sure about that. The events of the last war themselves reveal how thin was the veneer of our civilization. We have only to reread and contemplate those memorable lectures which were given to this Academy of Medicine by Dr. Leo Alexander to remind ourselves that science and morality do not necessarily go hand in hand. In our own generation we witnessed bestial cruelty, not only as an occasional morbid aberration, but rampant and impassionate. Therefore, in contemplating the advance of science, we cannot, but feel, occasionally, somewhat chastened.

But I am digressing here. My subject is the physical diseases of men and not the diseases of civilization. They—the diseases of civilization—are the affairs of the philosophers, not of the physicians. Or indeed, if you care to carry the responsibility still further back, it is the affair of the universities that produce the philosophers. If the universities cannot produce these wise contemplative men whom we call philosophers, or if they won't produce them, or if they have forgotten how to produce them, then society must invent new cultural institutes superior to the universities.

Returning to my subject, the point I wish to make is this. While we have done a great deal to conquer disease, we have done so by mobilizing forces and by creating instruments for this conquest. We must constantly be on the alert, keeping these forces mobilized, making new instruments, and having them always at hand. They must—these forces—be constantly alert in trying to see the changing character of disease, in trying to foretell what new tricks Nature may have up her sleeve.

I shall make the claim that one of these instruments must be, at all times, engaged in trying to see disease in what I have called its local setting, that is, disease as it is occurring in a local community, disease seen against the background of the local economic conditions, disease as it affects or as it is influenced by local conditions of life, that is, local culture. Some may call this social medicine or environmental medicine, but I prefer to call it just plain medicine.

Now, let us look back for a while and see what have been the forces and the instruments by which the control and conquest of disease has been gained. I shall stick here for a moment to the military metaphor and say that these forces have been like three brigades in an infantry division, or like the arrangement, as far as I remember it, of the British Army, like the three branches of a division, A, Q, and G: one concerned with the training of personnel, another concerned with supplies, and another concerned with fighting the battle. While using this metaphor, I wish to suggest to you that these three forces, which I shall shortly describe, with all their instruments, must work closely together. They may indeed criticize each other occasionally and benefit by that cross-criticism, but in the end they must in this way work together, they must know how the other works, although each has its own responsibility.

Before describing what I believe to be the three forces which must be constantly mobilized to be aware of the prospects of disease in the community, I must explain that my observations are based entirely on medicine as I see it in my own country, medicine as I have experienced it in England. Whether or not these observations have any application to any other country, I am not prepared to say.

Now, these three instruments which in any modern, complex Western society I believe to be necessary are, first, the universities in our midst. I think, alongside of them I would put the big research foundations, because in some respects their work is close to a part of the work of the universities. The second category is that tremendous force in the control and conquest of disease, namely, the medical profession itself. And thirdly, as another instrument engaged in this, I would place quite squarely the government of the day, whether it be local government or central government.

Each of these, as I say, has its own responsibility, but each must adjust its responsibility to fit the other two. I do not think that disease is likely to be kept under control unless each of these plays its own appropriate part. This means, in the last analysis, that each must have good leadership by wise men exercising wise judgment. It will be no good winning a tactical victory on the one front and losing it on the other two.

About the responsibilities of the universities and, as I have suggested, the research foundations, there will, I think, be little argument, but it is perhaps profitable occasionally to remind even the universities of these responsibilities. I think the first responsibility, if it is not going to be too whimsical to define it in this way, of a university is to be a university. That is a place where the criticism and evaluation of ideas is being continually carried forward, where nonsense can be exposed for what it is, where the intellectual virtue of sincerity of mind is fostered and transmitted, the transmission usually being a process carried out by the companionship between teacher and student. The university works and does these things by the processes of scholarship and research.

In medicine, universities have two other responsibilities. One is the selection and the education of men for the profession of medicine, and the other, in medicine, as in all other subjects with which a university should be concerned, is the opening out of new fields of knowledge for exploration and inquiry.

And, finally, as to the responsibility of the profession, again, I think, there will be little argument. It is responsible for the maintenance of the practice of medicine, for the application of knowledge discovered in research in the practice of medicine. There are, however, two other requirements of the profession: that it shall maintain a professional ethos, a standard of conduct within the profession which the profession sets itself; and it should maintain—otherwise it will not be a profession—professional freedom, which means, in my interpretation, the freedom to do what it ought to do in the way it considers best.

Now, let me say here that whatever divergences of view there may be in Britain about the organization of the professional practice of medicine, there is, I think, no doubt in the mind of any responsible person, probably of any political party, that the medical profession should not become a completely salaried service. It is understood that the profession, to remain free and therefore responsible to its obligations, should be, to that extent, self-managing. And it is indeed so—whatever misinterpretations may be made—that even under the new health service, it is not a salaried profession.

Now, about the responsibility of the third force, that is, government, for the control of disease, there may be some divergence of opinion. Some, perhaps, will say that government should keep out of it entirely and leave it all to the profession, but that is, I would submit, at least in my own country, regarded as a very extreme, perhaps outrageous view. The history of medicine in Britain over the last hundred years shows that government indeed has a responsibility in medicine and in medical care. The argument is not, should it play a part? The argument is, how should it play a part? How far should it go in playing a part? For I personally take the view that the government of a country, a complexly organized country, has not only the duty but the right to see that medical care and the control of disease, along with other social services with which it is competent to deal, are adequate for the nation's welfare.

So far I have taken a somewhat broad view of the responsibilities of medicine, and I must now take a more restricted view and describe my own experience, my own responsibility in the work I do, as I see it. It is, naturally, a local view and a personal view. If it were not, and if it were, as we say in the laboratory, a high-power view, it must be remembered that it would be colored with my own creations.

I work in the field of pediatrics. I do this work as a university man. It is my sole profession, therefore, to be a university teacher, a university researcher, and to do those other things which are expected of a university man. That I know, and I must acknowledge I feel greatly privileged. And, as every privilege in life carries an equal obligation, I must, from time to time, examine my obligation, and it seems to be the law of obligations that they go on increasing as one gets older.

Seen in this light, and considering the need, as part of my observation as a university man to be looking forward to fields of knowledge which may have to be extended, we can see what a wonderful record pediatrics has had. To the science of medicine alone, it has made extraordinarily great contributions. It was first in pediatrics that the application of modern chemistry to medicine was fostered. It was through pediatrics that the science of nutrition was first applied to human welfare. Pediatrics was among the first of the clinical subjects to link itself to preventive medicine. And nowhere was this better exemplified than in the City of New York in the hands of Dr. Holt, Sr., who played such a part in founding the specialty and the subject.

In spite of the technical difficulties of pediatrics, the difficulties of diagnosis, which were well expressed by an English physician when he said, "There is no branch of medicine in which experience is more necessary than in pediatrics, but no branch in which experience is more difficult to come by"—in spite of these difficulties, clinical pediatrics has advanced miraculously in this century. But this advance has been along the well-worn paths, the paths of clinical observation, clinical science, careful study of people in hospitals and in outpatient departments, the use of laboratory tests, the use of morbid anatomy, as we call it, the technics for the prevention of infection, either by immunizing processes or by the building of the kind of institutions in which cross-infection will not readily take place.

These, as I say, have been the well-worn paths of clinical study. The results are seen, of course, in pediatrics and the precision of diagnosis now available in disease, the quickness of diagnosis reached by modern tests, the extraordinary fall in infantile mortality rate. In the beginning of this century, in big industrial cities, one child out of five would die before the age of twelve months. Now it is less likely to be less than one out of four hundred. Twenty-five out of a thousand is about the level.

Another result of pediatrics has been the elaboration of institutes of various kinds and of institutions in which pediatrics may be carried out.

A third result, one which I think has some bearing on the subject, is the rise in the authority of the trained, professional man, the pediatrician, and the nurse. And what I hope in a moment to examine is whether this has not, in some fields, been carried too far.

We see pediatrics established as a highly technical branch of medicine, a whole army of eager men and women to advise women in the care of their children, sometimes having to carry the responsibility of taking those children into institutions for treatment. And therein many of these men and women are continuing their researches in the diagnosis and treatment of disease.

Now is the time to ask: where does pediatrics go from there? Has it gone too far in some direction? Are there new fields to be explored? Are there new instruments of exploration to be invented?

In my own attempts to answer these questions, I have turned in two directions. I assume that aside from whatever institutions, such as hospitals, may be necessary for normal conditions, that is, for the treatment of disease which cannot be treated at home, the chief instrument for child welfare in modern society is, or should be, the mother, and that the chief instrument for child development should be the family. I am not gainsaying the value of the hospital or other institutes, and I am not gainsaying the value of schools. But to develop these latter instruments to the disadvantage of the others, may indeed be a thing that has to be examined.

I have asked myself, should not pediatrics now turn itself to an objective study of these instruments? This, I know, is coming very near to anthropology. Nevertheless, if pediatrics, public health doctors and educators are creating their own institutions, they must ask themselves, what effect are these institutions and these instruments going to have on maternal capacity and on family technic (which to me is the same thing as family culture)? Are we going to revive Plato's idea, Rousseau's idea, that the state, or an organized profession working for the state, can do better in the care of the child than the parent himself? This is not to suggest to you that not all of Plato's ideas were necessarily good.

In my own city we have made an objective study of the domestic care of premature children. We have been able to demonstrate that in the case of all premature babies, at least those over the weight of three and a half pounds (within the terms of the definition, between the weights of three and a half pounds and five and a half pounds at birth) at a cost which is one tenth the cost of institutional care, we can get the same results by training and mobilizing some people to undertake the domestic care of the premature in their own homes.

I must here remind you of a local scene in England

which might not be familiar to you. In my own city, 57 per cent of the babies are born in their own homes, and only 43 per cent in hospitals.

Also in maternity hospitals and in a hospital we have created, for the last twenty-five years mothers have come in to undertake the nursing of their own babies. So the child may come from the operating room and be nursed in his mother's arms. Also, through the study of the homes of some people, we have been making observations on what might be called the filioparental reactions of the mother: her emotional reactions to the situation, her sense of achievement in experiencing success in the care of her child, particularly of caring for it through an illness, and the extent to which this experience and this sense of success brings about her own maturity as a woman.

I have heard it said, for example, by some of my colleagues that they can, in a street car, talk to a woman on a general subject and after two or three minutes' conversation, noting her responses, say whether she is a woman who has had this rich kind of experience and the sense of success in the bringing up of her own family or whether she has had an opposite experience. They go on to say that the street car is not named "Desire."

Another interesting feature is that there is also a field of adaptive physiology that is capable of study. We have noticed, for example, and confirmed—we have control observations—that for the woman who bears the responsibility for her sick child (this is more true at home than in the hospital) as long as that child is sick and constantly in need of attention, her sleep requirements are extraordinarily low. She may, throughout the nursing or a difficult illness, lasting a week or more, require no more than two or three hours of sleep and yet be alert for the remaining hours of the day. That is true as long as the baby is in physical contact with her. Remove the baby from her by sending him to the hospital, and she will fall into a profound exhaustive sleep.

Another adaptation we have noticed is that a woman's sensitivity for sound, particularly the sound of the voice of her own child, is far greater when that baby is very young than it would be at other times, or later, and it certainly must be within the observation of you that it is far greater at those times than is the sensitivity of the male parent.

These are indications of a kind of study which I think we need now to be carried out in a scientific manner, preliminary observations having been made.

Lastly and quite briefly, I come to another instrument which we have tried to develop, one by which we have tried to see disease, as I said, in its own setting, that is, in its proper perspective. In medicine, if we rely only on the hospital ward for our observations, only on the outpatient department, only on the laboratory, and only on public health statistics, we may be failing to see disease in its proper perspective.

To do this, some five years ago we took a sample of the community in which we live. To serve our purposes it was necessary to get this sample in a manner that represented all social classes in the right proportion. Our object was limited and quite simple in the beginning. It was to get this cross-sample of a number of babies in the community, because knowing, as we did, that respiratory illnesses in the first year of life, pneumonia and diseases like it, were very prone, quickly afterwards, to produce permanent damage of the lung, we wished, out of that sample, to take only the babies who had had these illnesses and study those babies for ten years, following closely, by the method of natural history, what the sequence of their respiratory diseases and lung diseases might be later in life. It took us a year to design the experiment, to train the workers, to collect the sample, to get it, become intimate with it, and then to find desertions in high number from the sample would have invalidated our results. From the statistical point of view we required about 1000 babies. So within the inner parish of the city, that is, within the area comprising 300,000 inhabitants, we could expect about 6000 births a year. So we collected our sample by taking every birth in the city during two months of a given year. It was a year of high birth rate, so eventually our sample was 1142.

I may here explain that it was designed with such care and done, I think, with such delicacy, if I may use that word, that we have had only four desertions in the sample of 1142, although the experiment did not end at the end of a year. We became so fascinated with the picture of life as it is lived, the diseases that go on in the family, studied that way, that we have continued the observations and are likely to continue them for another five years.

What, then, are we seeing? Through this instrument, what can we learn? In the first year, as I say, four people deserted. Some migrated, and we were not able to follow them. But even the reasons they migrated and went to other communities are an interesting bit of social history. What surprised us was the vast quantity of illness in children in an industrial town. Of the 1142 children, 44 died, which was about the expected number, but 947 of them required medical attention for illnesses in their first year of life. I admit some of these illnesses may have been transient, a short febrile cold, but some of them were indeed much more serious. It did put into the right perspective the different kinds of infectious illnesses to which children in that very sensitive period of their life are liable. It showed that the pattern of disease is indeed changing. The percentage, for instance, of infectious illnesses in that first year of life was not highest among such things as measles. It was in this field: pneumonia, severe kinds of bronchitis, and what we call acute respiratory illnesses, which represented 50 per cent of the total illnesses. Twenty-two per cent were represented by septic infections and their consequent results; only 11 per cent by the infectious gastroenteritis which a hundred years ago, fifty years ago, used to kill so many thousands of children every summer. Whooping cough, about which there used to be so much concern, was responsible for 10 per cent, measles only 4 per cent, tuberculosis 1.3 per cent. In this way we were then seeing disease in its true perspective.

I do not wish, nor do I think it is in order, to go into the technical details of the spread of disease within the family. But it has given to us certain indications as to why certain families are prone to certain diseases, and it has revealed to us that very often an infection in an older person will assume one form, in a middle-aged person another, and in the baby another still.

However, leaving aside these technical details, you may be more interested to hear some of the other sides of the study. We have used this instrument to give us a view of the medical services which are available to the community, to give us a clear, precise, objective view of how the people use the medical services; to give us the necessary view at a time like this when there is so much emotional conjecture going on about the medical services; to give us a view as to how good those services are or are not.

We have made a study of the reaction of children to their

stay in a hospital by examining them to ascertain how they behave when they come home. That is giving us, so to speak, a basic view of our own activities.

But perhaps one of the things that will interest you most is a study of maternal capacity. We have had to define this in a way that may sound to you a little loose. To define satisfactory maternal capacity, we have used a woman who, living in the circumstances she does, is able to provide effectively for the welfare of her children. This requires diligence, intelligence, sacrifice, love, and all the other things that go for that maternal capacity. We call such persons "copers." At the other extreme, we put people who are inordinately defective and in whose care it is almost unsafe to leave children. Those who are extremely defective we call "non-copers." They are, in the ordinary word, sluts. Perhaps I might explain that, having cross-divided our sample into the five social classes which most sociologists use in their categorization of the social classes, at least one of these sluts is in the higher social class.

In between those we have two other varieties: one we call people who are variable in their capacity to cope, and those who, though not seriously defective, dangerously defective, are yet unsatisfactory.

Having made this study, and having become very intimate with our sample, the figures are these: that of the 1142 (fewer now because of deaths and removals) only 2 per cent of the community in which I live and work are in the category of being severely defective in maternal capacity; 9 per cent are to some extent unsatisfactory but not dangerous; 5 per cent are variable (that it, with a little help, they get on very well, a little good neighborly help); and 82 per cent are completely satisfactory.

Now, if it ever were possible in social medicine, environmental medicine, or in the social sciences, to get a quotient in a community like this which represented the true capacity of mothers in a community with regard to their children, and were it possible to go on making a graph of that over the years, or were it possible to compare that index figure of one culture with another, one town with another, I think you would have an instrument that would tell you where your civilization was going. But I profoundly believe that the technics of culture are made by men and are transmitted by women.

In this way, a study which started off from a simple inquiry, to find why the Newcastle babies were so readily prone to be diseased, has ended up with a picture of a community, its way of living, its culture, its attitude toward its institutions. All of this, I believe, has given us teachers a wider perspective and will, no doubt be used to the benefit of our students.

It may be necessary for me, when you hear these figures, to explain a little of the background of the culture of this community. We are lucky in studying a community which has had practically no immigration, no mass migration, at any time in its history. It has also not suffered from the other extreme disadvantage of depopulation, such as happened in some of the Hebridean Islands as a result of living under economic circumstances in which most of the males had to leave the community. Population studies in those circumstances usually reveal that it is the most eager, the most adventurous, and therefore the best material that tends to emigrate.

So it has been an advantage to study a community with a culture going back more than a thousand years in that part of England where Christianity first rose, hardened by a thousand years of tribal warfare, in which there never has been a subservient peasant population; where, over the last four hundred years, there has been a slowly expanding industry in shipbuilding and coal, and the transmission of coal and the exporting of coal, which has absorbed nearly all of the male labor. There will be, inevitably, a few immigrations which come from marriage.

But it is against that background that I see my pediatrics in the community in which I live, and I have come to the conclusion that pediatrics must continue, as it obviously will do, to carry the responsibility for the earlier recognition of disease, cure of disease, and research in disease. It must continue to carry the responsibility for the prevention of disease so far, particularly, as it can be prevented by child health services. I think it now must concern itself with the culture of the community in which it lives, linking itself here to the educationalists, perhaps pointing out to the educationalists that its views are a little better than the educationalists' views may be as to what is, indeed, the background of the welfare of children.

Here I must confess that, glad as I am to accept this opportunity to come to New York to a meeting like this and an occasion like this, what I have to say concerns only the community in which I live, and if the instrument which I have briefly described has any application, it would have, indeed, to be modified to the community to which it was being applied.

But unless we can, through succeeding generations, supply to the community, year by year, children who are sensitive, tough, healthy, and courageous; children not afraid whimsically to examine what their educationalists are doing to them, not too subservient to the enthusiastic technician who wants to safeguard their health, and not too prone to the blandishments of the popular press—unless we can, in each generation, supply children of that kind, I have very great fear that the culture which I, at least, am interested in might deteriorate.

For that reason, I say, pediatrics or some part of pediatrics must go outside of the formalized fields of prevention, treatment, and cure. And I don't think attempts to define it as social medicine, as my dear friend John Ryle tried to define it, can be quite sufficient. Pediatrics comes down to a study of all those processes which safeguard the welfare of children, and particularly one which has been neglected to the present—the technic of motherhood.

Editor's note: Sir James Spence's address is here published as he delivered it. His unexpected death prevented a revision of the text. A fuller account of the work to which he refers in his lecture is now available in the book, *A Thousand Families in Newcastle-upon-Tyne* (Oxford University Press).

THE BIOLOGY OF ETHICS

R. W. Gerard, M. D., Ph. D., D. Sc.

PERHAPS YOU have decided that there is no serious mismating of the words in the title. To a great many people, however, the combination in one sentence of "biology," a science, and of "ethics," more usually associated with religion, would seem a bit out of line. At least people regularly do laugh when I tell them about a paper, written some years ago by a colleague of mine, entitled, "On the Religious Convictions of Cockroaches." This was published as a perfectly serious paper in a biological journal. The author employed all the proper paraphernalia of scientific procedure: he developed a hypothesis—that roaches should have a religion of one sort or another; and he devised a technique of testing for it—assuming that under conditions of extreme danger an individual would reveal his major belief. He got a glass tube about a yard long and an inch in diameter, put a hundred roaches in the center of it, and placed at one end a card with a cross on it and at the other, a card with a crescent. Then he lighted a burner under the middle. After enough trials to get statistically valid results, which were summarized in impressive tables, he concluded that cockroaches were 48 per cent Mohammedans, who went to the crescent; 49 per cent Christians, who went to the cross; and 3 per cent atheists, who died where they stood rather than turn to any religious symbol!

In a more serious vein, perhaps some of you would have been as surprised as I when, seeing the title of this address in the printed announcement, I thought I'd better check in a dictionary the correct definition of ethics. I confess to some amazement on finding the definition, "the *science* of moral duty; the *science* of ideal human behavior and aim." Incidentally, the word itself comes from a Greek sound from which also our word "custom" has come—certainly a pragmatic origin for the word "ethics." Also, the roach story is not so outrageous as it may seem now. The great mathematician Napier, to whom we owe logarithms, in all seriousness argued in his day that locusts were Mohammedans.

Even in Biblical times, though, and on matters of theological import, the experimental method was apparently acceptable and was used. Shirley Jackson Case, former Dean of the University of Chicago Divinity School, has evidence for this in his excellent book on the *Origins of Christian Supernaturalism,* which opens with the fine sentence: "The sky hung low in ancient days; and the traffic was heavy on the highway between Heaven and Earth." According to Kings 18:17-39, Ahab and Elijah, arguing as to the relative potency of their respective gods and neither being able to convince the other that Baal or Jehova, respectively, was the more powerful, agreed to an experimental test. Whichever god could most quickly bring fire to light the sacrificial offering, would be acknowledged the mightier. That, I think, is a perfectly good exemplification of the application of scientific method!

To return to our definition, when one brings in the terms *ideal, behavior* and *ends,* inevitably the conception of values is introduced. I think it may be useful to consider with you, in the time available, such topics as these: Are there values in this sense in science? Can science or anything else—religion, revelation, etc.—give us a certain understanding of what values should be, of what the right and good are (particularly the good concerns us here) and, finally, is there any way in which the concrete achievements of science—i.e., the growing knowledge and understanding of the world—enable us to make any statements at all in the realm of ethics? Can biology say: "Here is a line which looks meaningful in terms of ethics?"

I hope to arrive, and with your agreement, at a conclusion which is very satisfactory indeed: that biology or science, and religion—certainly the Christian religion—can say much the same thing. It is important to make sure that we have no misunderstanding, that we recognize that they are coming to these conclusions by quite different methods. I shall, therefore, take a little time before plunging explicitly into the matter of ethics, to discuss what science is and the relation between science and religion.

Science I talk about with some confidence; that has been my business for a good many years. Of course, by science I do not mean just the collective work or product of those people who happen to labor in departments, institutions, or laboratories, which are given the label of some science or other. Science is much more pervasive and inclusive than that would imply. Essentially, science is tested and organized common sense. But I would add the codicil: Our common sense today is very heavily tinctured by the accumulated results of science; particularly in the last three centuries, but actually ever since that time in the Greek era, in Hellenic civilization, when the intellectual processes of mankind made a pretty clear break with preceding attitudes. In earlier periods, the myth-making or mythopoeic mind, as it has been called, regarded the whole universe in personalized terms, as "I" and "thou." Everything was a spirit of some sort, to be propitiated or affronted, as the case might be. Then developed the impersonal attitude of "it," essential to the recognition that caprice did not dominate natural events, but that there was a regularity in the universe which could be depended upon. This is part of our common sense of today.

Science is also an attitude, a procedure, and the results of these, summed up in a sentence: Science attacks and solves problems by imagination, based on sensory evidence and, to use Coleridge's lovely phrase, "curbed and ruddered by reason." It is a particularly important and distinguishing aspect of science that all it does is somehow curbed and ruddered by reason.

Science is a human creation, like art. In fact, the talents involved in the successful pursuit of science are not very far removed from those used in the profession of architecture. Perhaps science involves more of the concrete ingredient than does pure art, but it is very close indeed to architecture in this respect. It is not entirely a poetic figure to speak of building more stately mansions in science, as it is not in architecture, however figurative it be for the soul. Science has, as does art, very great beauty. It has intense aesthetic values, even more of the spirit than the senses. Beyond the pretty pictures one can see through the polarizing microscope, as an example of the science appreciation now being popularized in mass magazines, even beyond a new volume on pictorial art by a leading artist built upon pictures of scientific objects taken in the course of normal scientific activities, there exist the deeper beauties of harmonic relations and elegant reasoning and deep understanding. But this is too long a story to develop now. Science also has values and it alters human life not only in practices but in attitudes. Science adds mechanism to understanding; and so, utility to truth. It supplies rational values and contributes to the true and the beautiful and to the good or useful as well.

To some extent, I am throwing out phrases and terms, hoping that some will catch your imagination and bring you some feeling of what science means to the scientist. Of course, one cannot really appreciate a major activity of man without living it; still some one or other of these views may carry significant meaning. Let me put it this way: Science is not a body of fact and doctrine; science is a way of life. If research were to stop now, in a few years we would still know all the facts we know today—indeed some "facts" we now know would have been proved wrong by the research. Nevertheless, our knowledge would have died; it would have turned to dogma; it would no longer be science. And I suggest that perhaps this is the touchstone which separates living dedication, whether it be to a religious idea or a national group or a scientific attitude or to any other intellectual or emotional subject, from dead creed. A living, growing discipline is under constant and free inquiry and flickers with new insights; when questioning stops, as a result of some kind of authoritative clamping down, the stuff congeals into a cold body of dogma. I have always loved that magnificent admonition, of Fouchet, I think, "Carry from the altar of the past the fire, not the ashes."

At a different level, science is an autocatalyst in human evolution. A catalyst, of course, is an agent which speeds change; an autocatalyst is an agent which not only speeds change, but produces more of itself so it progressively accelerates the speeding of change. Science disturbs us more and more, faster and faster, making social change or evolution occur at an ever-increasing rate. This you may regard as desirable or undesirable; it is indubitably happening.

Finally, I would like to characterize science in reference to certain pairs of opposing terms, without making value judgments on these pairs at the moment. Science is not like the formal, ritualistic, dogmatic type of religion, which is, of course, *absolutist*. Science, first of all, is *empirical*. Second, it is *operational;* one does things to find out further answers. The best antonym, I suppose, would be *revealed*. Science is *public;* the conclusions and convictions reached are subject to check by any other person who cares to go through the evidence or the experiment. The experiences of religion are essentially *private* and individual. Science is *cumulative;* there has been a progressive widening and deepening from its inception. Religion is *acculturated;* it varies, but not in any linear fashion, with time, place and community. Science is *universal,* religion is notoriously *sectarian*. And, finally, science is *rational,* religion more *emotional*.

Two of these points seem to me of especial significance. One is that science will not accept absolutes. It insists that all it knows, or thinks it knows, is relative and subject to further change with advancing information. The other has to do with the methodological or value precedence, as a source of knowledge, given to sensory experience and reason, on the one hand, and to revelation and belief, on the other. In science, reason has top compulsion over any outside authority. For many religions, of course, this is not the case.

So much for the detour into science as such. In developing the main theme, I am going to allow myself a certain amount of quotation from my past writings, partly to save time, partly because I cannot easily improve on these statements.

"The scientist would place reason in the highest priority, certainly as regards anything at the public level of inter-communication, which involves joint human decisions. The situation is perhaps different when one recedes into the privacy of the individual. For any one individual, his beliefs, whether they are rational or not, however they have been attained, even in a subjective vision which others might show was a manifestation of delirium, are often more imminent and compelling than his reason. But these remain with such a surround of affect only for him as an individual . . . A person's private feelings—his appreciation, belief, ecstasy—are of little and rare concern to others, however overwhelming to himself, except as they guide his actions. Reason is public and permits co-understanding; a person's insights, ideas, thoughts, can generate co-understanding across centuries and hemispheres. Art and religion are concerned mainly with private feeling, science with public thinking. Revelation can have no collective weight. As soon as the issues arise at the level of human communication, whenever people are trying to influence or convince one another, then the scientist would say that action based on reason must take precedence over that based on any other impulsion. Unless cumulative reason is held superior to individual inspiration, all of man's knowledge and achievement is imperiled.

"And only science is truly cumulative and universal in human history. Art, religion, culture is individual or local in time and space. Shakespeare's writings did not enable his followers to write even better than he; ethical beliefs and moral practices are different for great groups of mankind and at different epochs for each group; visiting or eating or dressing is performed in accord with the shifting dictates of custom and fashion. But Newton could truly say, 'If I saw further, 'twas because I stood on the shoulders of Titans.' And Russian as well as American guns fire in accord with the same laws of ballistics."

This potential conflict between the rational and the doctrinaire attitudes deserves another word or two. I am far from sure in my own mind what the present status is in our Western World, as between them. Father John Murray made an impressive statement in 1949: "I think sometimes that Newman had a prophetic moment when he spoke of the 'stern encounter' that history would see, 'when two real and living principles, simple, entire and consistent, one in the Church, the other out of it, at length rush upon one another, contending not for names and words or half-views, but for elementary notions and distinctive moral characters.' The two principles, he said, are, 'Catholic truth and Rationalism.' "

Perhaps the principles in conflict are even less limited. Compare Thomas Huxley's, "God, let me face a fact though it slay me," with Martin Luther's, "That silly little fool, that Devil's bride, Dame Reason, God's worst enemy." But today most theological thinkers find a place for reason, and scientists are more in harmony than in conflict with the deeper insights of religion. I quote again from Case, the eminent theologian, who traces the long history, from Greek times on, of the changing attitudes on the relation between the supernatural and the rational, "Not all [Greek] philosophers were thoroughgoing naturalists, but the tendency of all philosophical thinking was in the direction of reducing the domains of the supernatural . . . Although Christianity appropriated large areas of contemporary gentile culture, it still kept intellectualism in bondage to religion. This outcome was not a peculiarly Christian development, but its vogue was greatly accelerated by the conception of education that ultimately came to prevail within Christianity . . . It was now thought to be the supreme duty of the philosophers not to question the validity of the myths but to affirm their divine character. Creative mental effort had thus been virtually eliminated from the sphere of religion, and the dominance of faith over knowledge remained unchallenged.

"Of the mind's scientific quest, by which new and valid wisdom is acquired through observation of nature or the reading of immediate experience, the Christian philosopher who remained orthodox could have no genuine appreciation. That spirit of scientific research which had gradually developed among the Greeks until it ultimately produced an Aristotle, failed to find a home in the intellectualism of the ancient church . . . The theologians of the church never lost sight of their inherited conviction that faith should precede and transcend knowledge and that no knowledge was valid that did not agree with traditional beliefs. Since these were guaranteeed by revelation, they were superior to any form of human wisdom; the supernatural mind was thought to rule supreme over the mind of man . . . By the beginning of the twelfth century the rights of reason as a guide to Christian thinking began to be revived. At first the motive was the defense rather than the criticism of tradition, but even to admit the need and the propriety of defending Christian belief by human reason, apart from the compulsion of revelation, meant a virtual infringement upon the prerogatives of the supernatural."

One can find today a wealth of statements by eminent

churchmen in the vein of the latter statement from Case. Let me read you one more, by Edward Scribner Ames, also a distinguished member of the University of Chicago Theological School: "One of the greatest obstacles to this process of developing the goods and conditions conducive to better values is the conception that significant values are not indigenous to human experience, but belong to a transcendental realm, as in idealistic theories, Platonic theories and in traditional theological theories. The assumption that values already exist, that supreme ends are already formulated, inhibits the experimental effort to seek values through human intelligence and experience. This attitude has been overcome in the natural sciences where methods of experimentation have gained results and encouraged further inquiry.

"An empirical statement of religious values in the terms here indicated would bring them within reach of intelligent and practical development. So long as religious values are conceived to be transcendental they remain inaccessible to any intelligent criticism and cultivation. In an age when intelligent criticism is being applied so fruitfully to other interests, the failure to apply it to religious values removed religion farther and farther away from the common life, and to many people makes it seem negligible or worse."

I trust that my remarks do not make me seem hostile to religion, because that is not my attitude. May I quote from myself: "The University of Chicago's Alma Mater contains a line praising 'Her faith that truth shall make men free.' This might be taken as the basic ethic of modern science. Greek philosophy urged love of truth. Christian philosophy centers on 'Love of Man.' Science hopes to serve man by applying reason critically so as to increase understand-

ing and to engender wise actions . . . If one takes the
Graeco-Christian virtues in more detail, science still seems
'in tune.' The 'natural' virtues of wisdom or prudence,
fortitude, temperance, justice, patience, and humility, and
the 'Christian' virtues of faith, hope and charity are pretty
much all involved in the pursuit of science. Wisdom is
sought, temperance (tolerance) is fostered, justice is demanded in handling evidence and patience in acquiring
it, humility is engendered both by the immensity of knowledge and the greater immensity of ignorance, and faith in
uniformity and reason is implicit in all scientific activity,
as is hope of human betterment. Finally, service to man is
a continued consideration."

The religious facet of humanity is just as important as
the rational and each has its appropriate place. I would
sum up my own conviction by saying that religion is absolutely essential, or at least the emotional underlay of
religion, for there must be the belief in something, a desire
to work toward something, if man is to act at all. But the
direction in which he acts, the ends that he should seek,
are more likely to be given him by science than by any
other approach.

That brings me rather sharply to the question of the
values of science. I have spoken of truth being "a good."
This is not, of course, something proven by science; it is
something assumed by science, a matter of belief. It is shot
through all the activity of scientists; without such a belief
they would be quite unable to pursue their goal of trying
to find out truth. Yet it is not something in any way unique
to or indigenous in science.

Perhaps one would also be willing to accept, as a value
rather more centered in science, that existence itself is
good—there is at least the argument that, without exis-

tence, nothing can be good. In this connection, especially with the swelling criticism of science, indeed of rationalism, it is well to remember that, even if one unreasonably blamed all the casualties of the World Wars on science, the score would still be very favorable. X-rays alone saved incomparably more lives in the first half of the century than were lost in World War I, and penicillin has already saved untold more lives than were lost in World War II. Science has, of course, enormously increased longevity; decade by decade, the average life span has lengthened, and so rapidly that new sociological and economic problems, and psychological ones too, have arisen. Is increased length of life therefore bad?

Science also has something to say about the value of pursuing a goal of purpose. Purpose has been a particularly troublesome matter for biologists, and rather especially for physiologists, because it so often gets smuggled into our thinking unintentionally. One easily says the body does this or that in order to achieve something; but such a purposeful or a teleological "explanation" tends to close inquiry. The modern reaction has been so vigorous to this that professionals hardly dare use the notion of purpose. But much of what happens in living systems is really understandable in terms of the goals of physiological adjustments; these have a purpose, a utility, an adaptive value —whatever term one wants to use. The important thing is to get clues from the adaptations as to the required processes, then turn attention backwards to find what mechanisms operate them. So both the teleological and the mechanistic approaches are important in the biological area, perhaps more than in all others. As one famous physiologist last century said: "Teleology is like a mistress;

31

something that the physiologist cannot get along without but does not like to appear in public with."

Let me give some instances of what is meant by bringing in values. "All structural development and physiological activity of individuals is a similar succession of solved problems with shifting values. Blood is shunted to the muscles when one runs, to the gut during digestion; to the skin 'to nourish' it, yet from the skin which may be sacrificed, 'to conserve' body heat. A hand is jerked reflexly from a hot bar to avoid injury, but it will grasp the same object reflexly 'to maintain' balance. Almost always the physiologist first sees meaning in phenomena in terms of such purposes; as analysis proceeds he discovers new phenomena which enable him to think upstream in time, in terms of mechanisms. There is no reason to view man's purposing differently, it is only more difficult to emerge from the immediate internal view of it."

In the present day and age, moreover, we are so keenly aware of deliberately building "purpose" into man-made instruments, not only for the radar trailing of and automatic firing at airplanes, but more constructively into calculating machines, manufacturing controls and other mechanical brains, as they are fondly called by the press. The same principles are clearly present in "purpose"—called, if one prefers, "negative feedback"—in activity of the machines or the subhuman organism, and there is no reason to think it different at the human level.

Another quotation: "When man, proud possessor of an overstuffed brain, calls the brain the most 'valuable' organ and himself the highest form of life, he does well to suspect himself of anthropomorphizing. Valuable by what criteria? Animals can at least live without brains, they die without many other organs. But when he discovers, in many animals, that during starvation all organs waste away, are used for food, except the brain and heart, which are fed by the others; that a special reflex device is built into the arteries to the brain so that, within the limits of possible adjustment, the brain is insured its full blood supply whatever happens elsewhere; that the brain is more elaborately protected from injury than any other organ, even than the growing embryo, for it, like the embryo, is floated in a shock-absorbing fluid and, unlike the heart, is completely encased in bony armor; that success in winning habitats and capturing food parallels the development of the brain more than any other attribute: when man discovers these facts, he can feel distinctly more secure in his value judgment about the brain and so about his position. Not only man's mind, but his body and other animal bodies 'value' the brain."

The next aspect of values and ethics, particularly concerning ethics, is the question of "should" or "ought"— the idea of moral duty earlier quoted in the definition. Can science say anything at all about these imperatives? In one sense, and a very important one, yes. If a number of observations—say, on the height or weight of a growing child made week by week—are plotted as a regular curve, the next is expected to fall along that curve. It *should* be there; and if it isn't, one would say with considerable certainty that something untoward had happened to make the child's development abnormal. There is the "shouldness" that regularity should continue. When the chemists found an empty place in their table of the elements, as lined up by recurrent or periodic properties, they said there *should* be a chemical in that place; and in due time all the empty boxes were in fact filled. We all say the sun *should* rise at such and such a time tomorrow.

Actually, the expectation of continued regularity in the world has a deeper and more important significance, for it is built into the very structure of the nervous system itself. "Such truths are universal and constant in the species, are not consciously recognized or are at most adumbrated only after the most sophisticated delving, and they operate automatically to delimit the realm of thought. They are the 'truths' no mind is free to reject. Thus, it is not logic but physiology which makes us anticipate that regularity encountered in the past will be continued into the future. This property of the nervous system is clearly demonstrated in the formation of conditioned reflexes, in rats as well as in man, and is prior, not posterior, to any verbal axiom." When the same concatenation of events has occured a number of times, the nervous system expects it to be repeated; when the bell rings with each feeding, after a while the bell alone comes to induce salivation—there is no logic or reason or ideation about it. Regularity anticipation is just built into the nervous system.

Values, as I pointed out while describing science, are certainly not absolute; neither science nor anything else can give us absolute values. "The postulates of ethics (or religion) are of a very different character. From varying sets of philosophical (and empirical) assumptions, each moralist and his followers derive, most logically enough, ethical conclusions which differ in detail or in toto from those of others, yet for each of which is claimed the authority of intellectual compulsion. The mere existence of such differences refutes this claim. When great separate blocks of mankind, not occasional aberrant individuals, disagree upon the existence of a God, how can either position be a matter of valid inner certainty? . . . Science does not accept with final assurance that anything is good, or beautiful, or even true. It rejects absolutes. It depends on reason and particularly on that experience which comes ultimately from the senses. You will recall Leonardo da Vinci's statement: 'All knowledge is vain and erroneous excepting that brought into the world by sense perception, the mother of all certainty.'

"Aristotle, in reaction to Plato, likewise emphasized the importance of the senses, and it is the very essence of science to give sensory data a priority of compulsion over any other route to knowledge. To say that the physicist's picture of matter is far from our naive perception of validity is only to say that his senses have been sharpened, not that they have been superseded—as Mars is a point to the eye, a disk to the eye plus telescope. As Charcot well said a century ago; 'Disease is very old and nothing about it has changed. It is we who change as we learn to recognize what was formerly imperceptible.'

"A rational, or scientific, ethics can only be on the public level of intercommunication and agreement. It cannot be circumscribed by or built upon any fiats of innate a priori knowledge of right and wrong or of anything else. It cannot accept any intuitive certainty, any categorical imperative of duty, any revealed will of God, or love for Him, as its base or end. It cannot rely on a reward in the hereafter for virtue in the here-now. It must be empirical. It must seek ever wider and deeper roots in biology as the store of physiological and psychological knowledge grows. It must recognize and measure and compare the drives which determine conduct, not assume them. Studies on the relative rates of learning by rats when spurred by attainment of rewards or avoidance of punishment; on the dominant choice made by monkeys as between a mate or a banana, and the conditions which modify it; on the direction of change of a play group of children when run by an adult leader functioning as a democratic colleague or as a benevolent dictator; on the behavior patterns induced in rabbits by sex hormones or those attending the menstrual cycle of women; on the delusions or compulsive acts in the insane and neurotic; on the factors in the social milieu which make the psyche of the New Englander different from that of the old Englander of common stock, or of the Indian peon of present Mexico so different from his Toltec ancestor—such studies and thousands like them will answer the question of motives and sanctions for human conduct.

"Science continues to widen and deepen its generalizations, even to ethical problems; but any answer which is inherently beyond the potentiality of science is also beyond the possibility of reliable collective knowledge. Man, individually or collectively, must often act, must answer questions, with no assurance that his conclusion is correct. Well and good, even incorrect action generates new experience and permits improved understanding. But it is a sign of childhood, in the individual or in the culture, to believe one's fancies. The adult attitude is to face our present limitations with courage and our final limitations, as these are established, with renunciation.

"If the advance of science replaces sureties with uncertainties it is still better to recognize and admit our ignorance than to claim knowledge we do not possess. If our sacred cows of belief and convention cannot stand the light of reason they are sickly animals. Do you maintain that science has undermined the foundations of ethics, I reply 'Only of false ethics.' There is no conflict between the true and the good, any more than between the true and the beautiful. Whichever idols have crumbled with the growth of science were made of clay, and it is well to have cleaned out the debris. Religion is struggling to establish new ethical values; surely science, which has faith in truth and honesty, in patience and order, strains at her side. Perhaps, even, the new ethics will stem from science directly."

It is sometimes held that science destroys values. Yet Hitler and Stalin, who have certainly been against the important values of our culture, have also violated the bases of science and were brutally anti-scientific in orientation. A comment by the great physicist, Tyndall, on the Germany of a century ago, is timely: "It was really with the view of learning whether mathematics and physics could help me in other spheres, rather than with the desire of acquiring distinction in either science, that I ventured, in 1848, to break the continuity of my life, and devote the meagre funds then at my disposal to the study of science in Germany.

"But science soon fascinated me on its own account. To carry it duly and honestly out, moral qualities were incessantly invoked. There was no room allowed for insincerity—no room even for carelessness. The edifice of science had been raised by men who had unswervingly followed the truth as it is in nature; and in doing so had often sacrificed interests which are usually potent in this world. Among these rationalistic men of Germany I found conscientiousness in work as much insisted on as it could be among theologians. And why, since they had not the rewards or penalties of the theologian to offer to their disciples? Because they assumed, and were justified in assuming, that those whom they addressed had that within them which would respond to their appeal. If Germany should ever change for something less noble the simple earnestness and fidelity to duty, which in those days characterized her teachers, and through them her sons generally, it will not be because of rationalism. Such a decadent Germany might co-exist with the most rampant rationalism without their standing to each other in the relation of cause and effect."

Huxley also made a comment in 1886, in reply to a prevailing attack upon science, that deserves repetition: "The truth is, that in his zeal to paint 'Materialism,' in large letters, on everything he dislikes, Mr. Lilly forgets a very important fact, which, however, must be patent to every one who has paid attention to the history of human thought; and that fact is, that every one of the speculative difficulties which beset Kant's three problems, the existence of a Deity, the freedom of the will, and immortality, existed ages before anything that can be called physical science, and would continue to exist if modern physical science were swept away. All that physical science has done has been to make, as it were, visible and tangible some difficulties that formerly were more hard of apprehension. Moreover, these difficulties exist just as much on the hypothesis of Idealism as on that of Materialism. . . . Thus, when Mr. Lilly, like another Solomon Eagle, goes about proclaiming 'Woe to this wicked city,' and denouncing physical science as the evil genius of modern days—mother of materialism, and fatalism, and all sorts of other condemnable isms—I venture to beg him to lay the blame on the right shoulders; or, at least, to put in the dock, along with Science, those sinful sisters of hers, Philosophy and Theology, who, being so much older, should have known better than the poor Cinderella of the schools and universities over which they have so long dominated. No doubt modern society is diseased enough; but then it does not differ from older civilizations in that respect."

My own view is still that one "cannot prove that the

scientific view of the universe is the best or the final metaphysic which man will reach, or that truth is a crowning value. But I do maintain that this approach, of those man has tried, has led to great and progressive change in human affairs—mental as well as physical—and that, until an approach more satisfactory by empiric standards arises, or the limitations of the present one are clearly demonstrated, man had better 'Hold fast that which is good.' "

This is not to say that science encompasses all of man's concerns. Its aim is limited to understanding only; not appreciation—this is the province of the fine arts, although science may one day explain it; not use—this belongs to the applied arts and technology, although science creates these; and not action—here is the drive of religion, although science had better guide it.

The content of science is also limited, to the class and the public realm, leaving aside the individual and his private world. Private experience is prepotent to the individual, but science builds only on material of demonstrated collective validity. But it does not follow that a single solar system, a unique history of the earth or of living beings or of mankind, an individual patient or one of his dreams, or even a particular poem or painting cannot be tackled scientifically. For each individual is a member of many classes and even its uniqueness may be defined and derived from their intersections.

The area of science has also been limited in the past and is believed by some to be bounded for the future. But it has burst each assigned boundary so far and I see no reason to doubt that it will continue to. Science applied to the earth but not the heavens, then to the nonliving but not the animate, then to the functioning of organisms but not to their origin, then to the body but not the mind, then to the individual but not the group or society, and to mechanisms but not goals or purposes or ethics. Perhaps some domains of human interest will remain outside the scope of science; but if any questions of understanding are unanswerable by the advance of science, they are unanswerable to collective man.

At last I turn to the specific question of a biologic ethics. Many theological guesses about the right have been overthrown in the past and it seems safe to say that, on any point involving the nature of the world, the findings of science will overcome the dogmas of superstition. Contrast with the efficacy of penicillin that of a Roman health formula: "Depart, whether produced today or aforetime, whether created today or aforetime; this plague, this pestilence, this tumor, this inflammation, these goiters, these tonsils, this bunch, these swellings, this scrofula, this blotch, I call forth, I draw out, I exorcise by means of this magic from these limbs and marrow." Penicillin works better.

But the wise shepherd of souls, like other artists, can often point the way for the more ponderous march of science. "Artists, especially poets and other writers who deal with man's inner life (including religious leaders) have contributed greatly in noting and clarifying the phenomena ultimately to be analyzed and synthesized—as the naturalist-observer has supplied the raw factual nuggets which were beaten by the theorists and experimenters into such syntheses as evolution, and, if science denies absolutes, it may still provide vital support to such great and pervading insights. . . . If absolute and eternal moral laws are discarded, the alternative is not ethical chaos. If, perhaps, the perspective of a billion years or more of the history of a million kinds of living beings gives some empirical cues to practical morality, we may still salvage a workable ethics from the wreckage."

I must here briefly develop the idea of a system, an org, as I have called it, composed of subordinate units which interact together to form a single greater whole, like atoms in a molecule or cells in a multicellular animal. Such orgs, if examined historically or in terms of evolution, cosmic, not biological, evolution, have shown a regular progression from homogeneous units, all doing more or less the same things and in effect competing with each other to do the same job, to differentiated units, structurally and functionally distinct. The separate parts became specialized, each doing one portion of the total job needed, the whole group at the same time becoming ever more tightly reintegrated, interdependent. No one unit could any longer get by on its own, so to speak. Instead of competition between like units, there is increasing co-operation between unlike units, with the whole system much more tightly cohesive. The growth of co-operation or cohesion is marked in evolution of organisms or solar systems.

In the biological realm, one sees this particularly strongly. I must omit the powerful evidence for regarding groups of organisms, various types of societies, as epiorganisms; but ask you to accept that an epiorganism is indeed a biological entity, an org built of individuals as subordinate units, just as a man is an org, built of cells as subordinate units. Man as an ultimate individual is thus in conflict with himself as a penultimate unit in a group. Some of the implications of this dichotomy, and some conclusions regarding human beliefs and social evolution are condensed in these final quotations.

"The basic conflict, seen alike in all persons—children and adults, men and women, whites and blacks and reds and yellows, rich and poor—is that between the inborn and the inculcated needs or urges or drives or desires as they are variously called. The selfish, hostile, competitive, demanding drives are the most elemental and depend on the ancient segmental nervous system; they are largely summed up in the term self-love; they are the subjective aspect of the struggle for individual survival and success or power, presumably throughout the living world and certainly throughout the mammals. The life and death battles between males for mastery of the herd offer perhaps the purest manifestation of this. Such inwardly directed 'libido' is in necessary conflict with the conditions of group living in any form of society and is opposed by the influence of the social milieu.

"But men also cooperate as units in a group, as seen at all levels, from the sacrifice of a parent for a child or a friend for a friend, to that of the patriot for his country or the martyr for his cause. This behavior makes for the survival of the race or group rather than of the individual and makes for advance rather than security. It is dependent on the new suprasegmental nervous system, the cerebrum, which alone makes possible such abstractions and ideals as justice and truth, and the psychological counterpart of which are the drives towards love and altruism, the superego of the psychoanalyst or the conscience of common expression.

"It is not unimportant that one of the steady evolutionary trends has been towards better care of the young. This is true in plants and sub-mammalian animals, mostly on a structural basis, such as stored food in a seed or egg, although some insects make or capture food for their offspring by 'voluntary' effort of the whole individual rather than by the 'automatic' action of growing cells or organs.

. . . But in birds and especially in mammals this care is extended. In the latter the nursing mother remains with her young, a family is formed, psychological as well as physiological help is given, things are taught, the parent 'voluntarily' sacrifices for the children. This 'deliberate' care of the young (in contrast to simpler structural or 'instinctual' mechanisms) increases through mammals with the growth of the cerebrum, and it is disrupted or abolished in proportion as the cerebrum of the mother animal is operatively injured. In contrast, the 'narcissistic' behavior of an animal is not destroyed but is actually exaggerated when the cerebrum is removed, it goes only when the phylogenetically older hypothalamus is injured.

"Selfish and altruistic impulsions are thus ancient and both have evolved progressively. The latter, however, have gained relatively to the former and in more recent animal history have increased notably. They have flowered with the actual growth of the cerebrum, so predominant in man, and they have been fostered by all social milieu for they are necessary to group living. But these are the social virtues; and again biology finds progress in cooperation of the parts in the whole, this time the species or the community or the epiorganism.

"Man as an organism competes with every other man, but men as units in an epiorganism cooperate for the welfare of their society in its struggle with its environment— biotic or physical. This is not unique at the societal level but is, I think, that guiding thread we hoped to find interwoven in the pattern of all evolution. The direction of evolutionary change is consistently from the more homogeneous, with different structural regions performing like functions in 'competition' with one another, to the more differentiated and reintegrated, with different regions specialized for separate functions, division of labor, and co-operation of all parts in terms of the whole. This is as true at the levels of protoplasm, cell, tissue, organ or multicellular individual as it is at the levels of family, hive, herd, clan, community, state, or whole species.

"The same duality of man as an individual whole and as a unit in a group runs through all aspects of human interest. This is seen at the philosophical level in the extreme positions of endemonism and utilitarianism, or of individualism and collectivism. It is seen in political theory in its extremes as anarchism and totalitarianism, with democracy somewhere between; and in economic theory as laissez faire and absolute socialism, with planning again intermediate. In jurisprudence, the law of the mob, might is right, and the law of agreement, the lex juris; in religion, the multiformity of particular sects and the world ecumenical movement towards a unified religion; and in art and esthetics, the variegated local customs in dress and the like as against the strong tendency towards world uniformity in these matters, are all further examples of the same antinomy and of the trend of movement. In general, mankind is moving from freedom to exist towards freedom to live as human beings; man's political organization is moving from many sovereign nations to a single world state; and man's ethical orientation is shifting from an emphasis on 'mine and thine' to an emphasis on 'our.'" Science gives only one answer to Cain's question, "I *am* my brother's keeper." It is certainly satisfying that, on this basic issue, science and religion come to the same conclusion. Now let me summarize.

"Biology recognizes at all levels of organization the co-existence of equilibrium and change, of passivity and activity, of being and becoming. It sees in protoplasms of the cell, cells of the organism, and organisms of the epiorganism, competition and cooperation, selfishness and altruism, hostility and devotion; and it insists, further, that the grand panorama of the living, and the narrower vista of the thinking, show alike the same motif, of change—in the direction of greater selflessness of the units as they are parts of ever more integrated wholes.

"There is a clear and usable ethics based on empirical observation of what the world is. It is not spun by the mind alone, from postulates which inevitably turn out to be disputable and which can often be traced to particular emotional sets in their positors. Rather it has behind it a body of coherent and universely accepted evidence which points a clear direction and impels movement along it.

"As man's science, his accumulated and organized and tested knowledge, leads him to state ever more sweeping generalizations, with ever more confidence in their enduring validity, about what the world is like and in which way it is moving, he approaches closer to an empirical answer to the grand problems of philosophy. Certainty of absolute values we shall never have, but certainly science will supply values founded on an immense knowledge of the universe, wide in space and deep in time, values more weighty to all men than those imposed by a particular period and locale on some of them."

Science has given us a Utopia of means, it may yet give us a Utopia of ends. And the religious spirit must urge men toward it.

THE NATURAL HISTORY OF
NEUROTIC BEHAVIOR

Howard S. Liddell, Ph. D.

EIGHTY-NINE years have elapsed since Thomas Huxley reviewed the evidence as to man's place in nature. Today, the need for a realistic reappraisal of the place of human nature in nature may be imperative if man is to survive the consequences of his own ingenuity.

A recent symposium on the biological aspects of mental health and disease (Kruse, 1952) disclosed a formidable array of facts concerning the operations and capacities of the human organism, and demonstrated the biologist's present command of the most refined techniques of the physical sciences.

Parallel progress has been made in the social sciences. We have witnessed rapid developments in group dynamics and communication, and the sociological orientation toward mental illness is illustrated by the phrase "neurotic personality of our time." Moreover, psychiatrist and anthropologist now co-operate in the field and in the hospital in the analysis of the cultural determinants of personality structure.

With all these new scientific insights, biological and social, concerning man, we are, nevertheless, involved in a dilemma which cannot be resolved by putting a hyphen between words, or compounding them, as in the magic concept *psychosomatic*. We still look upon man with one eye as an animal organism, and with the other eye see him as a person or socius. Binocular fusion does not take place. How are we, as scientists, to regain that stereoscopic view of man which artists have never lost?

Perhaps the answer is to be found in applying the old-fashioned disciplines of the naturalist to the problems of human and animal behavior, and especially to problems of emotion.

The argument of the discourse this evening will be that man's neurotic behavior, like his vermiform appendix, has its animal origins. Further, his primitive impulses to behave repetitively and compulsively can be controlled only by a fuller understanding of the biological origins of his impulses to behave repetitively but *creatively*. That is to say, we must inquire into the animal origins not only of the neurotic process but also of the aesthetic process. A deeper knowledge of man's natural history—of his place in nature—should aid us in attempting to understand why one person must continually wash his hands, or avoid high places, while another must be forever writing poetry or painting pictures.

To the sincere observer of living things, no detail of behavior, either of animal or man, can be neglected as of no importance; since high spirits and cheerfulness as contrasted with gloom and despair are not unique attributes of human conduct, Charles Darwin (1896) found worthy of scientific note the customary emotional display of his dog whilst going for a walk.

"I formerly possessed a large dog," he writes, "who, like every other dog, was much pleased to go out walking. He showed his pleasure by trotting gravely before me with high steps, head much raised, moderately erected ears, and tail carried aloft but not stiffly. Not far from my house, a path branches off to the right, leading to the hot-house, which I used often to visit for a few moments, to look at my experimental plants. This was always a great disappointment to the dog, as he did not know whether I should continue my walk; and the instantaneous and complete change of expression which came over him as my body swerved in the least toward the path (and I sometimes tried this as an experiment) was laughable. His look of dejection was known to every member of the family, and was called his *hot-house face*. This consisted in the head drooping much, the whole body sinking a little and remaining motionless; the ears and the tail falling suddenly down, but the tail was by no means wagged. With the falling of the ears and of his great chops, the eyes became much changed in appearance, and I fancied that they looked less bright. His aspect was that of piteous, hopeless dejection. ... Every detail in his attitude was in complete opposition to his former joyful yet dignified bearing."

This anecdote illustrates one variety of *self-perpetuating behavior*. The dog likes to go walking with his master and seeks occasions for doing so. He even contrives, as we all know, to elicit situations in which going for a walk may be repeated over and over. *The activity is its own reward.*

Twenty-five years ago I observed another variety of this self-perpetuating or self-rewarding behavior in my experimental sheep. At that time I was rigorously scientific, or to put it bluntly hide-bound, in my thinking, so I made note of, but did not publish, the following observations.

The sheep were trained to run an out-of-door maze of three parallel alleys eighty feet long. Released by a falling door from a small enclosure, the animal found its way down the central alley and then had to discover which of the two outer alleys led back to food and sight of the flock in the barn through a grilled door. The other alley was blocked at its end.

All of the sheep easily learned to find their way through this simple maze. Then the problem was made more difficult. The animal now ran the maze four times in succession but the position of the outer blind alley alternated from trial to trial. The sheep reaching the end of the central alley must, to avoid the blind alley, turn right on the first trial, left on the second trial, right on the third, and left again on the final trial. This sequence was never perfectly learned by any of the animals even after three years of training.

All sheep alternated correctly on the first two runs but made an occasional wrong turn on the third trial and more frequently a wrong turn on the fourth and final trial of the day. In spite of its failure to master this routine each of the sheep habitually waited at the grilled door leading from the barn into the maze when I appeared to start the day's test.

As soon as an animal was allowed to enter the maze it hastily took a mouthful of oats from the food box but, without stopping to eat, walked briskly to the door leading into the starting enclosure and waited to be let inside. Its hasty nibble at the oats in transit resembled typical behavior at a cocktail party where appetizing morsels are perfunctorily selected and nibbled without interrupting the animated conversation.

At the end of each trial the same perfunctory attitude toward the oats box was observed. Often, the sheep coming out of the maze into the feeding compartment at once turned toward the door into the starting enclosure and, without pausing in its turning movement, rubbed its snout over the surface of the oats without taking even the smallest bite. The flock in the barn, plainly visible through the grilled door, was ignored by the sheep in the maze. Cutting off the view into the barn by closing a wooden storm door had no visibly disturbing effect upon the sheep preoccupied with its maze-running activities.

Thus the two rewards—the satisfaction of hunger and of the flock instinct, upon which I had relied to lure the sheep through the maze—were shown to be of negligible significance. A more disconcerting episode followed. One of the sheep who zestfully engaged in her daily explorations of the maze had a lamb. In deference to her condition we fenced this ewe with her newborn lamb in one corner of the barn. When the lamb was a few days old, the mother repeatedly bleated at me one day at maze-running time. I released her and the lamb from the pen and she ran at once to the entrance to the maze and waited there as she had formerly done on training days. I allowed her to enter the maze but kept the lamb in the barn where it threw itself against the grilled door, bleating lustily. It was in plain sight of its mother and only a yard away. The mother, however, completely ignored her lamb and resumed her business-like and deliberate running of the maze for the usual four trials. At the end of each trial she nibbled briefly at the oats in the food box but completely ignored her bleating and violently struggling lamb.

For this career-minded mother the protection of her young appeared to be less urgent than the exercise of her skill in running the maze.

During a period of six years I trained more than fifty sheep and goats to run the maze for the purpose of determining the effect of removing the thyroid gland upon the intelligence of these simple farm animals. In no instance did I ever observe behavior in sheep or goat which remotely suggested a persisting emotional disturbance as a consequence of failure to perfect the maze habit just described. The animal tolerated its frequent failures with equanimity and continued to practice its defective skill with zest. What amateur string quartet does not do likewise?

In these experiments the animal did what it wanted to do, not what the experimenter wanted it to do. As a physiologist interested in the effect of absence or excess of thyroid hormone on behavior I found this self-perpetuating activity of the animal in the maze most frustrating.

If a motor nerve is stimulated its muscle contracts. If a small quantity of adrenalin is intravenously injected, heart rate increases and blood pressure rises according to the amount injected. Observation of the stimulus-bound activities of tissues and organs gives the physiologist a sense of security since the accuracy of his findings increases with refinement of the control of stimuli. The conduct of the sheep in the maze was not stimulus-bound. Even if its behavior could, in theory, be reduced to a stimulus-response basis, it was certain that I was not in control of the stimulus situation but the sheep was.

In those years, little was known in this country of Pavlov's investigation of conditioned reflexes. It was, therefore, an event of major scientific importance when in the spring of 1923 Dr. G. V. Anrep, a former assistant of Professor Pavlov, delivered a series of lectures at the College of Physicians and Surgeons. He presented the details of the monumental conditioning studies which had been continued in Petrograd even during the war, revolution, and subsequent

Howard S. Liddell

famine. Dogs as well as experimenters were at times both cold and almost starved but, under the indomitable leadership of Pavlov, the work continued. I heard Anrep lecture, and he helped me plan my first conditioned reflex laboratory in Ithaca. At his suggestion, I visited Pavlov's laboratory in the summer of 1926 where I had the good fortune to meet our chairman, Dr. W. Horsley Gantt. To his single-minded zeal as a veteran investigator of conditioned reflexes I wish to pay grateful tribute.

Here at last, in Pavlov's method I discovered a means of analyzing sheep and goat behavior in a situation where the animal, through training, relinquished the spontaneity of action which had proven so frustrating in the maze-learning experiments. Its conditioned reflexes, positive and negative, were elicited by the experimenter. He gave the appropriate signals at *his* convenience and each conditioned reflex was *demonstrably* a stimulus-bound and relatively brief episode of activity. In the intervals between such episodes the well-trained animal maintained a state of quiet watchfulness or vigilance. We would experience in similar circumstances a state of psychic tension. I make this statement with some confidence because for many years we have made a practice in our laboratory of trying new conditioning experiments upon ourselves before subjecting our experimental animals to them.

In one of Anrep's lectures in 1923 we learned of Pavlov's new field of investigation—the experimental neuroses in dogs which developed as a consequence of difficult conditioning. He described an experiment performed in 1914 in which a dog, unable to discriminate a circle as signal for food from an almost circular oval as no-food signal, suddenly lost his poise and skill, attacked the apparatus with his teeth, barked violently and had to be kept away from the laboratory. He presented, according to Pavlov (1927), "all the symptoms of an acute neurosis." Following Anrep's visit, we began in 1924 a systematic investigation of conditioned reflexes in the sheep and goat which has continued without interruption to the present. The animals are conditioned not to food but to the forced reaction to a mild electrical startle-stimulus applied to the foreleg for a fifth of a second. We, ourselves, experience no more than a slight tingle when this feeble electric current is applied to the moistened fingertips but sheep and goats are always startled by this same mild, but abrupt, stimulus to the skin of the limb.

Early in 1927, one of the sheep which had been trained in the maze over a period of more than two years was brought to the laboratory for conditioning. It soon exhibited precise flexion of the foreleg at the sound of a metronome which had regularly signaled the application of the mild electrical stimulus. It remained quietly standing in the restraining harness between signals and, at the sound of the metronome, executed two or three precise flexions of the foreleg with a final brisk flexion at the application of the startle-stimulus. However, within a period of three days we increased the number of signals during each test period from ten to twenty, thus doubling the sheep's stimulus load. Quite suddenly the animal became agitated and like Pavlov's dog could no longer maintain its poise and skill. It became highly nervous even without signals and gave repeated small tic-like flexions of the trained foreleg. Moreover, it now resisted being led to the laboratory.

From Anrep's description of Pavlov's experimentally neurotic dog, we suspected that our sheep had developed an experimental neurosis. Further investigation during the next four years fully confirmed our interpretation and we

found that we could precipitate this chronic behavior dis-
order in any sheep by certain conditioning procedures
which I shall presently describe. During these four years,
three more sheep developed experimental neurosis. In each
case the abnormal pattern of behavior persisted for life.
Our first neurotic sheep, for example, lived to thirteen and
a half years and exhibited its chronic agitation in the
laboratory, barn, and pasture until the end.

In one case, the sheep's experimental neurosis was precipitated by the same procedure which led to the neurotic
breakdown of Pavlov's dog. A metronome, clicking at the
rate of 120 per minute, was a signal for the forced startle-
reaction, while 50 per minute was the signal for no startle.
The metronome at 50 per minute was increased to 60 per
minute as a negative (or no startle) signal, and by gradual
increments the negative rate finally reached 92 beats per
minute as contrasted with the positive signal of 120 beats
per minute. At this point, the experimental neurosis supervened. Both in sheep and dog the positive and negative
signals had become confusingly similar. The animal, because of its self-imposed restraint in the training harness,
could not avoid the demands of the stimulus situation by
escape, but must face the insoluble problem of Pavlov's
dog in distinguishing oval from circle or of our sheep in
deciding between the metronome at 92 beats and the
metronome at 120 beats.

In the free situation provided by our out-of-door maze,
or in the field, the animal can escape a confusing stimulus
situation by inactivity, detouring, or flight. F. Fraser Darling (1946) during his observation of a herd of red deer
in northern Scotland witnessed the behavior of these deer
in the wild state when subjected to confusing sensory cues.
He writes:

"Smell is by far the most meaningful sense in the lives of red deer. Their reliance on the information it conveys is absolute. When, for example, deer smell man, they do not wait for confirmation of the fact by the exercise of other senses; they move away. Localization of the source of the scent-exciting attention is remarkably accurate. Wind is naturally of great importance in the conveyance of scent but, if the wind is of such unstable quality that it is a succession of eddies from all points, the deer may be driven to panic by inability to localize the source of a disturbing scent. An incident occurred on April 14, 1934, which illustrates this. I was descending the quartzite cliffs of Coir' a' Ghiubhsachain, the wind being fitful from the west and south and the humidity high. Two stags were on the other side of the corrie approximately a half a mile away. Up went their heads, but they looked southwards and not at me. They wheeled with their noses towards An Teallach, back again, and over towards me. It was obvious that they did not know the direction or distance I was from them and I do not doubt it was my scent which had been carried to them on a most unreliable wind. They trotted uphill a hundred yards and tried the wind again by raising their muzzles to all quarters. Still they could not place me, and, considering the dull light and the distance, it was unlikely that I could be seen by them. They turned towards the Toll Lochan corrie and went over the rough ground at the gallop, then over some quartzite slabs towards Sail Liath. At that time there was a large snowfield on the north-eastern face of Sail Liath, topped by a considerable cornice. The two stags went into the snow, plunging upwards as fast as the conditions allowed. The deer are in poor condition at this time and their frightened movement severely winded the two stags. Outlined as they were against the snow, I could see through the glass the open mouths, the tongues prominent, and the breath coming fast. They plunged finally through the snow cornice, sinking to their bellies and once on the hard ground at the top they went quickly out of sight on to the Strath na Sheallag side of the hill. These two stags were not strangers to me, although I had but newly taken up the work, and it is unlikely they would have made such a long and difficult journey had I surprised them by scent and sight at a hundred yards' range. Had they seen me moving steadily at the distance they were from me at first, it is probable they would not have moved at all."

Here, as in the maze, we witness stimulus-elicited behavior but not stimulus-bound behavior. Having detected the smell of man but being unable to locate the source, these stags fled in panic. But having escaped, that was the end of the matter. Not so in the case of the animal restrained in the conditioning frame. When the positive and negative conditioned stimuli or signals become confusingly similar, the situation is radically different. Day after day the animal is subjected by the experimenter to these confusing sensory cues. Fight or flight is of no avail. The animal (dog, pig, sheep or goat, and we have investigated all of them) must maintain its state of tense but uncertain expectancy. This behavior is truly stimulus-bound and the *terminus ad quem* of such training procedures we have found to be "neurotic" breakdown.

Another regimen which inevitably leads to experimental neurosis is the one on which we now exclusively rely to precipitate these chronic disorders of behavior. The animal, restrained from locomotion by a strap around its middle, running through a cleat attached to the wall, soon gives up its struggle for freedom and maintains a state of vigilance or quiet watchfulness in expectation of what is to happen next.

If a metronome clicks for ten seconds and is followed by the usual mild startle-stimulus to the foreleg, the sheep or goat will soon begin to flex its forelimb in anticipation of this terminal event. Now, however, an added stimulus-binding of its behavior is introduced. Each day twenty metronome signals of ten seconds' duration are spaced exactly two minutes apart. Here, it is not the confusing of signals but the unrelieved monotony of signaling for ten seconds every two minutes day after day that eventually brings the animal to its neurotic state.

The full measure of the animal's self-imposed restraint in the conventional conditioning situation, we have come to appreciate only during the last two years in studying the sexual and aggressive behavior of the mature ram. When the immature male at three months is fixed against the wall by the web strap around the chest, he soon gives up his struggles and promptly learns to flex the foreleg at the sound of the metronome. Within a period of a few months this young ram develops a battery of motor skills or conditioned reflexes, both positive and negative. When he arrives at sexual maturity no changes are observed in his laboratory deportment. At the end of three years his responses to the experimenter's conditioned signals are not observed to differ from the responses exhibited by any sheep of like age whether female or castrate male.

However, if a ram one year of age with no previous laboratory experience is subjected to the monotonous regimen of signals every two minutes, his behavior during the early days of training is both dramatic and violent. At the metronome signal he vigorously butts the wooden partition in front of him, repeatedly paws at the rubber mat on which he stands, and bellows menacingly. He will instantly butt at the experimenter if he approaches closely enough. He never, in our experience, develops the poise and skill shown almost from the beginning of training by the sexually immature ram.

Instead, when subjected daily to the monotonous and rigid time schedule of signals just described, his sexually aggressive behavior is suddenly replaced by rigid immobility—a premonitory manifestation of the type of experimental neurosis with which we have long been familiar in sheep and goats and which we have called tonic immobility. At the signal, he now lowers his head and tenses the forelimbs but no sign of flexion appears until he is forced to flex the forelimb by the application of the electrical startle-stimulus at the end of the signal.

When I first witnessed this impressive display of agression by the mature ram in response to the conditioned stimuli, and sometimes spontaneously during the intervals between signals, Freud's (1932) graphic description of the id came to mind. He writes:

"We can come nearer to the id with images, and call it a chaos, a cauldron of seething excitement. We suppose that it is somewhere in direct contact with somatic processes and takes over from them instinctual needs and gives them mental expression, but we cannot say in what substratum this contact is made. These instincts fill it with energy, but it has no organization and no unified will, only an impulsion to obtain satisfaction for the instinctual needs in accordance with the pleasure principle."

It may seem a far cry from our barnyard laboratory to the psychiatrist's consulting room. Is it really so far? I venture the opinion that the simple experiments just described bring us to the threshold of fundamental problems of psychoneurosis; namely, the nature of the unconscious and the operation of repression. What are the biological origins of repression and the unconscious? By our easily reproducible techniques of stimulus-binding, the adult ram's seething excitement which welled up in unbridled pawing, butting, and bellowing was suddenly quelled, giving place to tense immobility. Moreover, when conditioning was begun as early as three months the ram upon reaching sexual maturity never manifested in the laboratory the aggressive behavior appropriate to the adult male. The vital machinery involved in clamping the lid upon the cauldron of seething sexuality and aggression in these rams has yet to be disclosed, but I believe that our experimental techniques will prove adequate to the task.

During the past five years we have been investigating another fundamental problem of neurotic behavior. This problem has to do with the influence of environmental stress upon the newborn sheep and goat. How early in life can experimental neuroses be precipitated? Secondly, what influence can the mother exert in protecting her offspring against the stimulus-binding procedures which inevitably lead to neurotic behavior in the adult sheep and goat? Our present tentative answers to these questions can best be given by reviewing recent case histories of two lambs and one kid based upon my own daily observations.[1]

You will remember that Freud (1939) believed the symptoms of a neurosis to be the consequences of strong impressions and experiences going back to early childhood, the period up to about five years. According to him the features that characterize the neurotic process—"the features common to all neurotic symptoms are first the at-

1 This investigation was supported (in part) by a research grant from the National Institute of Mental Health, U. S. Public Health Service.

tempts to revive the traumatic experience, to live once more through a repetition of it but, second, to remember or repeat nothing of the forgotten traumatic experience or impression. This negative aspect of the neurotic process is expressed in avoiding issues and often culminates in an inhibition or phobia. In brief, the neurotic process imposes restrictions of the personality and gives behavior the characteristic of compulsiveness."

Neurotic behavior is then both self-perpetuating and stimulus-bound. The stimuli, however, are the original injuriously intense experiences and impressions whose enduring traces continue to dominate or bind the individual's daily conduct, perhaps for life.

All three of our little animals were subjected to the same mild stress situation. However, in spite of its seeming mildness we had discovered that its daily repetition inevitably led to experimental neurosis. The lamb or kid was tested in a bare laboratory room ten feet square. A flexible cable suspended from the center of the ceiling was attached to a web strap around the chest, and electrodes from the cable were fastened to the forefoot. This cable served a double purpose. First, as the animal moved about the room it operated a lever system on the ceiling and by means of pairs of self-synchronous motors the animal's locomotion was recorded on the page of a notebook in an adjoining room. The total amount of movement could also be estimated from a pair of Veedor counters connected with the lever system. Second, through the cable the animal received its mild electrical startle-stimulus at the end of the conditioning signal.

In all three cases now to be reviewed, the stress procedure consisted in suddenly dimming the overhead lights for ten seconds as a signal for the startle-stimulus to the forefoot when the lights came on again. At each test period the animal was subjected to twenty of these brief periods of darkness spaced two minutes apart. This monotonous stimulus sequence was controlled from a central clocking device so that the observer might give undivided attention to the animal's behavior.

Darkness is a particularly effective conditioning signal since sheep and goat may literally be afraid of the dark. One bright February morning many years ago there was a total solar eclipse in Ithaca. I let our small flock of sheep out of the barn and they spread out over the small pasture to nose in the snow for blades of grass. As the light rapidly failed the sheep moved together into a compact mass and a ram took his station at the periphery of the flock. Then after total eclipse, the animals gradually spread over the pasture once more as the light increased, and resumed their grazing. Moreover, we have found from numerous experiments that for sheep and goat (unlike the dog) darkness is a more effective conditioned stimulus than sound.

The first case history is our most recent one. A female lamb was born last July 10, far past the usual lambing season. At four days of age it was brought to the laboratory room with its mother, the recording cable and electrodes were attached but no signals were given. When six days of age it was brought to the laboratory again and given its first training routine of twenty darkness signals. At the fourth signal it gave clear evidence of conditioning by assuming a rigid posture, and then backing away from its mother with small jerky steps at the eighth second of darkness. It had bleated but once near the beginning of the test period and for the rest of its training with the mother in the room it remained mute.

Its original conditioned reaction, body tensing, is seen

when one approaches the flock in pasture. Darling (1946) describes this same sentinel reaction in the red deer as follows:

"Let us note the reactions of deer at a distance of two hundred and fifty yards watching an observer walking along a footpath. At the first glimpse their heads are raised and the two forefeet come together. These two movements are synchronous. They stand motionless in whatever position they are and watch the person walking. As long as he keeps on walking all is well. They are not frightened, and they do not move. But if the observer stops, probably they will go. If he makes any stealthy movements within their sight such as crawling in the heather or getting behind a rock, they will certainly run away."

It is this primitive questioning, or investigating reaction, upon which all conditioned reflexes, or organized expectancies, are based and it is the freezing of this reaction which characterizes one type of experimental neurosis in our sheep and goats as we saw in the ram and as we shall see again later.

As might have been expected, the young lamb behaved at later darkness signals by crowding behind the mother, out of the observer's sight. He was sitting in a chair in one corner taking notes. Mother and lamb both stared repeatedly at the observer who did not startle them but sat quietly. Other reactions to darkness signals were jerky head movements followed by tentative stepping forward or backward. The most interesting conditioned reaction was seen at the eleventh signal of the first test day. It was repeated on later days and can be described as a "still reaction." The lamb remained absolutely motionless during the signal and flexed the foreleg only slightly at the electrical startle-stimulus at the end.

During the second signal the lamb continued nursing until its forced reaction to the startle-stimulus at the end.

On the twenty-second signal, the second signal of the second day, the lamb being but seven days old, the first precise flexion of the foreleg at darkness was observed after a latency of five seconds. This skilled response was repeated more and more frequently with less and less locomotion. According to W. T. James (1951), a correspondingly precise flexion of the forelimb in the puppy cannot be conditioned until sometime between the twenty-eighth and thirty-seventh day of life.

The lamb was trained daily for five days with its mother in the room, and on the last day gave four "still reactions." It was then ten days old and had been subjected to a total of 100 darkness signals.

These so-called "still reactions," with complete immobility, may derive from the young's reaction to the mother's danger signal in the wild state. Here again, it will be necessary to call upon the skill and knowledge of the naturalist for further information.

On August 13, at a month and three days of age, the lamb was returned to the laboratory for further stressful conditioning but now without the "protective" presence of the mother. It was subjected to seven test periods between August 13 and August 20. Then it was released from further work and will not be tested again until it reaches middle age, and for the following reason. On its third period in the laboratory it exhibited dramatic evidences of the experimental neurosis, but on the remaining four days of testing these signs had almost completely vanished. Our interest is to discover whether any traces of this transitory emotional disturbance remain when stressful training is resumed in two or three more years.

The "neurotic" flare-up began after the seventh signal and consisted first of small, brisk, tic-like flexions of the trained foreleg, long recognized as evidence of experimental neurosis in the adult sheep. During the ensuing twenty-four minutes 154 of these movements were counted in the intervals between signals, often attaining a tempo of a flexion every two or three seconds. Just before the nineteenth signal the lamb lay down and remained so during the signal, rolling a little at the application of the startle-stimulus to the foreleg. This is another characteristic manifestation of experimental neurosis in the sheep. The neurotic animal is sometimes found lying by itself on the barn floor after the daily test, the rest of the flock having gone to pasture.

While lying down, the lamb exhibited a third neurotic sign which we have come to recognize in both sheep and goat; namely teeth-grinding, or bruxism as it has been called. There are more than thirty mouth habits presumably of neurotic origin, such as lip- and cheek-biting, clenching or grinding the teeth which bring the patient to the attention of the psychiatrist or dental surgeon. We have recently begun to note in detail nose-licking, cud-chewing, teeth-grinding, wheezing and other oral manifestations in our animals under stressful training.

The remaining two case histories can be briefly summarized. We chose twin lambs, castrate males three weeks of age and subjected them each day to the stressful training imposed on the lamb just described. One twin was confined alone in the laboratory room while its twin, at the same time, was placed in the adjoining room with its mother, and the routine of twenty darkness signals per day was instituted. The lamb in the presence of its mother continued to explore the testing room in the intervals between signals, while the isolated lamb became more and more restricted in its activity, first, avoiding the center of the room, but finally staying in the corner near the observer's chair; then lying down, head on the floor with no observable reaction to the signal, not even ear movement. This lamb ground its teeth from time to time throughout training, and at the end of the thirty-second test period began grinding its teeth at cud-chewing tempo, but the cud was not regurgitated. It first began lying down following the seventeenth signal of the twenty-second test day, and on the very next day refused for the first time to follow its twin and mother when they were being led to the laboratory.

The tests were terminated after thirty-two days of training, the animals being put out to pasture. The twin trained in solitude died at age ten months, while the twin protected by the companionship of the mother during the stressful routine is in good health at a year and a half of age.

The final case history concerns twin castrate male kids in which the usual monotonously stressful training was begun at a month of age. One twin was trained in isolation, the other in the presence of its mother with results comparable to those just detailed in the case of the twin lambs. The isolated kid became more and more restricted in its movements, first staying against the walls and in the corners, but finally standing rigidly near the observer's chair and watching him intently. In this little goat, however, a striking manifestation of the neurotic pattern which we have called tonic immobility supervened. At the "lights-out signal" the kid lifted its trained leg in stiff extension from the shoulder, and if the electrical startle-stimulus was not applied to the forefoot the limb remained in stiff extension, slowly sinking to the floor. This young kid, like the isolated lamb, survived its training period only a few months.

Finally, in order to explore the influence of drugs, hormones, and other procedures on the experimental neurosis, it is now possible to train a number of sheep or goats at one time according to our rigid schedule of darkness signals by confining them with restraining straps to the walls of the laboratory and simultaneously recording the movements of their trained forelegs on a kymograph in a distant room.

A question may have occurred to you as I was describing our monotonous and rigid signaling routine which seems inevitably to lead to experimental neurosis. Could the animal be given "an instrument of freedom" by which it might escape the injurious results of this stressful regimen of training? What if the animal could avoid the electrical startle at the end of each signal by keeping the leg flexed until the signal stopped? In this case, it could control at least one stimulus binding its behavior.

For the past two years we have been training some of our sheep and goats to avoid the reinforcing stimulus or electrical startle to the limb by maintaining flexion to the end of the signal. *This procedure does not, however, enable the animal to escape experimental neurosis.*

One goat, trained for class demonstration to flex its forelimb at the buzzer in order to avoid the electrical stimulus, has now completed many months of testing without receiving a single terminal startle. However, its behavior is still stimulus-bound. This was illustrated one day when a new electric fence had been strung in the pasture. The goat approached the fence and brought its muzzle in light contact with the wire. At the shock, it wheeled and dashed away some yards, then turned to face the fence and deliberately flexed its trained foreleg in precisely the way it was accustomed to do in the laboratory at the sound of the buzzer.

Earlier this evening I contrasted the neurotic process with the aesthetic process; *compulsively* repetitive behavior with *creatively* repetitive behavior. Thomas French (1950) has recently expressed the same thought in a different way; contrasting needs with hopes. He writes:

"In the integration of goal-directed behavior needs and hopes evidently play complementary roles. They may be thought of as the poles, negative and positive about which all behavior is oriented. First of all, we seek to escape from painful tensions arising out of our needs, but our efforts tend to be focused more specifically upon positive goals based upon our hopes." Most physicians, of necessity, must be constantly engaged in the task of lightening the stimulus load of neurotic sufferers who cannot escape the continuing pain and fear arising out of imperative but unrecognized needs.

I believe that physicians and laymen alike should conspire in the task of understanding the aesthetic process better, in order that it may be employed as a therapeutic lever in raising man's spirits. Van der Horst (1950) has given this illustration of the operation of the aesthetic process:

"One of our children, a boy aged four years and two months, was drawing an immense number of circles; during this perservering occupation he was asked what he was drawing. He answered, 'I don't know; it isn't finished yet.' After a short time he made a number of dots in each circle and cried in triumph, 'Biscuits with sugared caraway seeds.'"

Howard S. Liddell

What I am thinking of as the aesthetic process is adumbrated in Pavlov's reflex of purpose, and is probably identical with Freud's concepts of sublimation and ego ideal. It has been characterized by theologians as devotion to matters of ultimate concern.

The enjoyment of Darwin's dog on going for a walk, and our sheep's zest in running the maze, should suggest to the investigator of behavior the necessity of discovering further methods for providing the experimental animal with "instruments of freedom"; with techniques or skills for escaping from, or mastering, the restrictions of a stimulus-binding environment.

If we can come to a fuller scientific understanding of how to alter the balance between stimulus-bound behavior and self-rewarding behavior which is also self-perpetuating, gloom and despair can be made to give place to cheerfulness and high spirits.

The thoughts of Charles Darwin (1896) on cheerfulness and high spirits may serve as a conclusion to this discourse. He says:

"From the excitement of pleasure the circulation becomes more rapid; the eyes are bright and the color of the face rises. The brain, being stimulated by the increased flow of blood reacts on the mental powers; lively ideas pass still more rapidly through the mind, and the affections are warmed. I heard a child, a little under four years old, when asked what was meant by being in good spirits, answer, 'It is laughing, talking, and kissing.' "

REFERENCES

Darling, F. Fraser (1946), *A Herd of Red Deer,* New York: Oxford University Press.

Darwin, Charles (1896), *The Expression of the Emotions in Man and Animals.* New York: Appleton.

French, Thomas M. (1950), Study of the Integrative Process: Its Importance for Psychiatric Theory. In *Feelings and Emotions,* ed. M. L. Reymert. New York: McGraw-Hill.

Freud, Sigmund (1932), *New Introductory Lectures on Psychoanalysis.* New York: Norton, 1933.

—— (1939), *Moses and Monotheism.* London: Hogarth Press.

James, W. T. (1951), Personal communication.

Kruse, H. R., ed. (1952), *Symposium on the Biological Aspects of Mental Health and Disease.* New York: Hoeber.

Pavlov, I. P. (1927), *Conditioned Reflexes.* New York: Oxford University Press.

van der Horst, L. (1950), Affect, Expression, and Symbolic Function in the Drawing of Children. In *Feelings and Emotions,* ed. M. L. Reymert. New York: McGraw-Hill.

ENVIRONMENT AND HEREDITY

Theodore H. Ingalls, M. D.

IN THE course of a Laity Lecture delivered here in 1949 on the subject of "Science Under Dictatorship," Dr. Leo Alexander referred to "the recent attempt of the Russian government to suppress the work of the Mendelian geneticists." Continuing, he remarked on "the similar trend of the Nazi government to extoll the significance of Mendelian geneticists and to suppress the critics of that branch of science."

"There is no doubt," said Dr. Alexander, referring to the extreme position taken by the Soviet geneticist Lysenko, "that the Russian government is playing down genetics because a society of its type needs a firm belief in the modifiability of human beings as a source of its morale. . . . In Nazi Germany the situation was reversed: their morale was based on a compensatory belief in innate superiority, which presupposed unmodifiability." These two contrasting beliefs, the one emphasizing only the inherited character of defects present at birth, and the other emphasizing only environmental influences as they act on the embryo, have been struggling with each other in a controversy which has been going on now for nearly two hundred and fifty years.

A debate of Lincoln-Douglas proportions occupied the

Academie Française from 1724 to 1743 on the subject of whether freaks and monsters were, or were not, preformed in the male sperm. In the first half of the nineteenth century Lamarck's theories on adaptation were advanced only to be countered later by Darwin's theory of natural selection. Then Mendel's magnificent discovery settled the matter so securely in the first half of the present century that Rosenberg could fabricate an imperial policy out of it for his Führer. Now Soviet Russia would swing the pendulum back through the full cycle. Both extreme viewpoints appear to be nonsense.

By way of introduction, I make no pretense of having mastered all the necessary facets of genetics, biostatistics, microbiology, biochemistry, epidemiology and medicine needed to settle the long controversy, nor of being prepared to roll a vast erudition together into one lecture as easily as my wife bakes a pie. Certainly no one man knows the details, nor has the experience to cope authoritatively with all the pertinent facts that lie outside his field of specialization. On the other hand, brave attempts to view the world have to be made from time to time, which is justifiable, providing the beholder continually bears in mind that he is looking at both a macrocosm and a microcosm, and with a sharply restricted field of vision. Examining this huge area of heredity and environment, I shall wear my own bifocals and peer out from the special viewpoint of gross malformations which are present at birth. I shall discuss first how woefully little we know about the inheritance of human malformations; second, some recent gains in understanding environmental features of the human problem; and third, recent interesting experiments that bear on both genetics and epidemiology.

I have stated that little is known of inheritable malformations, and yet textbooks are filled with accounts of them. Before accepting the family pedigree at face value, it should be clear that the function of a gene like the function of an atom cannot be witnessed but is demonstrated indirectly through what it does. Although the evidence that it exists is as sound as the evidence that proves an atom, the human gene cannot be examined macroscopically during life or even microscopically after death. The clinician studying the genetic background of cleft palate, malformed heart, or anemia due to Rh. factor has never seen the invisible gene of which he speaks so learnedly and so confidently. He asks whether the patient's father or mother, his brother or his aunt had cleft palate, congenital heart disease or anemia due to Rh. incompatibility. Affirmative answers to such primer-simple questions are inadequate and no more than indirect evidence to show that the gene plays a mathematically constant determining role. That cleft palate or some other defect occurs in each of identical twins does not prove this to be a simple matter of heredity. They do share the same genetic constitution and within the uterus both are supposed to share an identical environment. Yet cases are on record where only one of the two was born with cleft palate.

It is dubious scientific procedure to assume that complex defects of man are governed by laws that have served so successfully to explain fruit fly defects. To emphasize similarities between defective fruit flies and defective people is to minimize the gap between the two species and to ignore the intricate developmental processes of the human embryo from conception to birth. To conclude that complex defects like blindness, deafness, cleft palate, mental deficiency, and spastic paralysis are genetic "characters" because they repeat themselves in families is to confuse proof with assumption. Erroneous conclusions would be of no consequence, or simply ludicrous, were it not that they often have serious social repercussions. Books of a past generation, such as *The Jukes and the Kallikaks* and *The Mongol in Our Midst,* for example, were accepted all too credulously as scientific studies, and at their face value. Even today, I can find in excellent textbooks pedigrees of "mental deficiency," "spastic paralysis," and "hydrocephalus" with the unjustified implication that these are well-established hereditary conditions because they run in families.

Lest it appear that I discount the contribution of genetics to scientific knowledge, let me say that it is for lack of time that I do not list the many defects that are primarily inherited. An eminent mathematician-geneticist, Lancelot Hogben, makes my point for me this way:

"We do not, and cannot, transmit characters to our offspring. A character as such, is the end product of a vastly intricate sequence of reactions involving the impact of innumerable environmental agencies on a specific initial genetic equipment of the cells of the body. To discuss whether a character, as such, is inherited or acquired, therefore, shows a slovenly disregard for the semantic decencies. What we can discuss with propriety and lucidity is whether a particular difference between two individuals is, or is not, attributable to the different equipment the cells of the body possess in virtue of the material composition of the parent egg, or sperm."

Sunburn is a simple example of the intricate sequence of reactions which involves both the genetic equipment of a man and the environment in which he lives. Were the sun unknown, sunburn might be interpreted as a genetic disease of red-headed, light-complected, freckled, blue-eyed

73

Theodore H. Ingalls

people and most assuredly to run in families. Conversely, to reduce sunburn to a condition solely due to the sun is to ignore the constitution of the host and the contribution of the environment, whether that be tropical or arctic, sea level or mountain plateau. The agent, the host and the environment act together to produce the burn. Each component is an essential cause of the final effect, just as each of three bars must be in line to win the jack pot in a slot machine. To insist that only one bar releases the jack pot is missing the point. All three are needed, and when only two are showing, the presence or absence of the third becomes critical.

Interactions of the environment with the inherited constitution are easily shown after birth. For example, bleeders with hemophilia get along all right providing they suffer no bruises. The possibility that there are similar interactions in the period before birth has until lately been virtually ignored. That babies are born with anemia due to Rh. reactions with their own mother's blood is taken for granted, since blood tests show the condition has a hereditary basis. Although the adverse combination of husband-wife blood groups is present in about 13 per cent of marriages, relatively few offspring run into trouble. Sensitization is as necessary as inheritance. Continued fatalistic acceptance of Rh. anemia in babies would be like accepting sunburn as an inherited condition without studying factors of exposure.

The possibility that many congenital defects are acquired—that is to say, determined after fertilization of the ovum—was not seriously explored until the past decade. In 1940 Gregg, in work that is probably familiar to you, showed that German measles attacking a pregnant woman can cause blindness, deafness, heart disease, or even mental retardation of the baby. This discovery came decades after the recognition of the ability of syphilis to cause equally severe defects in the fetus. The lesson of congenital syphilis was overlooked, however, for life before birth had become a blind spot between the fields of genetics, obstetrics and pediatrics. The conclusion is inevitable that biology, obstetrics and epidemiology, genetics, embryology and mathematics are to be applied in concert to the problem of congenital malformations. High walls sealing off tight compartments are crumbling.

The original interest in prenatal malformations was through legend and superstition. A century before my father saw the famous Siamese twins, Eng and Chan, in Barnum's circus, the French scientist, Geoffroy St. Hilaire published a three-volume book on the subject of freaks. Two thousand years earlier the ancient Romans worshiped the two-headed God Janus and named one of the months in his honor. Cyclops was not venerated, for he was a monster like the minotaur, too hideous to be admitted into the natural order of things, although sirens peopled mythology in a graceful, acceptable manner. By and large, the birth of a monster was interpreted as an omen from the Gods— the portentous shadow cast before troubled events. Before the Romans and the Greeks the Egyptians regarded anencephalic babies, that is to say infants stillborn with a gaping defect of the skull, as the product of bestial mating of man and monkey. Indeed, the oldest known specimen was recovered from a sarcophagus reserved for the mummies of the sacred animals of the Nile.

These monsters, freaks and lesser malformations are not to be viewed as Nature's pranks of yesteryear, nor as the products of a vanished civilization like sirens and satyrs. Janus and Cyclops occasionally make their appearance in the lying-in hospitals of today, and what the ancients could have called faun we call Mongoloid—stressing the slanted eyes rather than the pointed ears. The present cost to society is to be measured not only in terms of the grotesque, that is to say in terms of the subjective amazement and horror of the beholder. The so-called "monsters" are to be measured numerically by the thousands among the aborted and miscarried dead, the blighted offspring of the country's pregnant population. The misshapen fauns carry their lesser defects and handicaps with them when they leave the bassinet, many for the state asylums and the homes for crippled children. These deformed beings do not happen without rhyme or reason. Different patients vary from each other as do different "stills" from a moving picture strip. They carry the message of a photograph, that here is the portrait of a person or process arrested in motion. The dynamic process that has been interrupted when identical twins do not separate is still the splitting in two of a single egg-cell mass to make two persons. This theme of untimely arrest of growth runs as a basic pattern through the whole of malformations before birth. To define cyclopia as a single eye is to oversimplify the problem. Gradations exist between pure one-eyedness and normal two-eyedness, even three- and four-eyedness. Arrests of growth rarely involve the whole body, more often a major segment such as the head, trunk or extremities, but the bulk of defects is to be found in localized and lesser abnormalities, like cleft palate, hernia, heart deformities and the like. Occasionally Nature lets loose in all directions and the result is a Mongoloid child, with a whole constellation of minor defects.

Mongolism was for many years called "Mongolian idiocy." A popular and long-enduring explanation for the condition is that of "defective germ plasm." This is a fence-straddling phrase. If due to defective germ plasm, what is the nature of the defect? What caused it? Did it exist incipiently when the ovum was fertilized (that is to say, was it predominently genetic), or was it subsequently acquired between the time of fertilization and birth?

The argument that Mongolism has a significant hereditary component finds little biologic support. Benda, for example, found that only two of 255 families having a Mongoloid child had a second. Moreover, Mongoloid patients do not reproduce. With the frequency of second occurrence as low as one per cent and with direct descent playing no part in propagation, the case for genetic causation is slim indeed. That Mongolism represents a specific mutation is scarcely to be considered because of the relative frequency with which the disease occurs—about once or twice per 1000 births.

On the other hand, when Mongolism is viewed as a problem of populations and not of individuals, when it is looked upon as a mass disease, new facts emerge in explanation of cause. Epidemiologic investigation follows a procedure not unlike that employed in the old game of twenty questions which begins "Is it animal, vegetable or mineral?" In the game of scientific inquiry, Nature herself is the master of ceremonies who answers the questions. Thus from an epidemiologic viewpoint when we ask "Does Mongolism occur among the progeny of older or younger women?" we get a good answer. The average age of mothers of Mongoloid babies is about 41 years compared to an average of 23 years for mothers in general. The risks increase with advancing years. The explanation awaits clarification. Age of itself is wholly inadequate in explanation of Mongolism, but age may well be a measure of chronic disturbances that contribute to causation. The game of twenty questions goes on, with the possibilities to be considered that poor function of the endocrine glands or involutionary changes in the uterus play parts. For example, the age group 40-50 marks a decade of beginning sexual involution. Disturbances of the thyroid gland are also more frequent among mothers of Mongoloid babies than among mothers of healthy babies.

Some 10 or 15 per cent of mothers of Mongoloid babies have an acute infection on or about the eighth week of pregnancy. On the basis of arrests of growth, I interpret this period as being critical for the production of Mongolism. These arrests have to do with malformations of nasal bones, palate, teeth, and middle phalanges of the little fingers. The list of stunted tissues could be extended, but at the risk of obscuring the import in a mass of detail. Above all else, the defective tissues of the Mongoloid baby are those which come into being at about the eighth week of intrauterine life, and here is the place to search for causes. I say causes, not cause of Mongolism.

If the gulf between the geneticist and the environmentalist is to be bridged, the concept of multiple causation will be the keystone. Failure to appreciate that the same end result may be due to a number of different causes or combinations of causes is a principal obstacle to a common meeting ground for physician and geneticist. In 1870 not everyone accepted Koch's demonstration that one kind of microbe could produce multiple, unlike diseases—that this little, red-staining tubercle bacillus could cause entirely different conditions depending upon the site of infection in the brain, lungs, glands or bones. A great German physician, Virchow, went to his grave refusing to accept the simple fact because it offended beliefs of a lifetime. The interpretation today is that Mongolism, cleft palate and other deformities have no single cause—that there may be as many causes as there are ways to break a leg. Evidence is now introduced to show that environmental injuries act with inherited and developmental features of the embryo to produce congenital malformations.

Continuing experiments since 1946 in the laboratory of the Department of Epidemiology at the Harvard School of Public Health have had to do with the effect of lack of oxygen on the unborn young of pregnant mice. In order to select a method that injures without killing the litter, a chamber was constructed to rarefy the air mice breathe. Housing the mother within the chamber is equivalent to transporting her to altitudes where life is almost, but not quite, impossible. Pregnant mice are kept in the chamber for a single period of five hours, an experience that approximates breathing air close to the top of Mount Everest, 28,000 feet high. Whether pregnant mice do or do not suffer lasting effects from this experience is not known, but a high percentage of the offspring are defective at birth compared with those not subjected to this environmental stress.

Under the conditions of the experiment, a wide range of deformities occurs, the nature of which are determined both by degree of oxygen lack and the time in pregnancy. White mice had severe deformities of the brain, skull and skeleton when the mother had too little oxygen on the eighth day of pregnancy. Cleft palate was a common result of exposure on the fourteenth day and a curious defect of the eye and eyelids—so-called open eye—when pregnancy had advanced about sixteen days. To attribute these various defects to mere lack of oxygen is oversimplification.

The experiments show that when the maternal upset occurs is just as important as what that upset is.

To state that two causes, lack of oxygen and particular stages in the development of the embryo work together to produce malformations is to reinforce the principle of multiple causation. The principle holds true for both cleft palate and open eye and still more—for these deformities occur after X-ray treatments, or vitamin deficiencies or chemical poisoning during pregnancy.

Since cleft palate occurs spontaneously in 5 to 10 per cent of the progeny of certain strains of mice, genetic factors in causation are introduced. There is no reason to believe, however, that a particular defect in a single gene is responsible for all naturally occurring cases of cleft palate among mice when, as has been demonstrated, the condition can be produced by numerous different environmental injuries in mice selected at random.

On the other hand, observations made with my co-workers demonstrate that genetic factors of the breed modify reaction of the embryo to lack of oxygen during pregnancy. Last June, we arranged to repeat the work just described, using so-called dba brown mice at the Jackson Memorial Laboratories. We used our own apparatus from Boston, the experiment was supervised by the same operator. Nothing was changed except the breed of mouse and the air of Maine for that of Massachusetts. Brown mice of the dba strain normally produce 1 to 2 per cent of stillborn or soon-to-die young with small to massive hernias. Mice placed in the chamber on or around the eighth day of pregnancy produced over 15 per cent of young with hernias. This deformity has not been observed in several thousand white mice embryos similarly treated. The probability is that constitutional susceptibility is inherited and that the specific defect is brought out by stress.

When I started to speak this evening, I spoke of a debate that had been going on for two centuries. The controversy started with differences of opinion and speculation over the causes of freaks and monsters—whether they were or were not preformed in the male sperm. When logic and science were substituted for speculation and metaphysics, the issue developed into whether environment or heredity determines that man's estate is getting better or getting worse.

The evidence presented here argues against either heredity or environment as a wholly determining cause of congenital malformations. The facts are that no sharp split is demonstrable between the embryonic host and its intrauterine environment. Environment and heredity are to be appraised as overlapping influences, with the first sometimes dominating a situation, and sometimes the second. A forced choice between extreme positions—Aryan racial supremacy in 1941 and Lysenkoism in 1951—is reduced to absurdity.

The time has come to subject to the hard rules of science and logic unsupported speculations on the causes of defects seen at birth. The clinician has too long had the obligation to prove that a congenital defect is acquired. Failure to do so has too long been considered evidence of genetic origin. The clinical case helps to point up the problem. Experimental genetics contributes to theory. Only through studying human populations—and this is what Dr. John Gordon has developed as "the newer epidemiology"—can we hope to prove whether or not forces shaping sweet peas, fruit flies, and white mice also govern the destinies of human beings.

Theodore H. Ingalls

Conventional distinctions between inherited and acquired disease before birth may well be modified, as future research makes clearer how both influences operate and how they may be controlled. In the present state of our society no reasonable hope is to be had that the heterogeneous selection of wives and husbands can be altered. I have yet to see the young couple introduced with the warning that the handsome man is Rh. positive while the girl in the dress with the green sleeves is Rh. negative. At present the value of human genetics is, to quote Professor Dobzhansky, "above all else philosophical in the sense that it strives to contribute towards man's understanding of the nature of life and of himself." We have important fragments of an understanding of the physical nature of man and his defects, and we know how to proceed with large-scale attacks against an adverse environment. Moreover, in the laboratory we have a model, a kind of universe in miniature, where the forces determining congenital defects can be isolated while details are dissected. Outside laboratory walls lies the real arena of life; the real challenge to use the forces determining health and disease to improve the quality of a newborn child rather than the quantity of our offspring.

CHANGING CONCEPTS OF CHILD CARE: A HISTORICAL REVIEW

Milton J. E. Senn, M. D.

O NE OF THE truly phenomenal developments in the United States has been the emergence of the social and psychological conviction which affirms that each child is a distinct personality and is to be so understood and treated. This conviction is in stark contrast to the view held earlier which represented the child as a being occupying a position subordinate to the adult. It is the purpose of this paper to describe briefly how this change of philosophy evolved, and how it is reflected currently in child-care practices and in trends in the fields of pediatrics, psychiatry and public health.

At the onset, there must be a definition of terms. In this paper the child referred to is an individual of either sex, who in age ranges from infancy into adolescence, and whose status represents the total aggregate of his participation in the affairs of our society—in the affairs of family, school, industry and the nation at large—each of which helped to mold and shape him, and was in turn influenced by him. The child will be spoken of as a person in general and composite terms. This is for reasons of brevity and does not imply lack of recognition of the existence of social status systems, and of subcultural groupings within the United States of America which give special significance to certain children, sometimes to the harm and detriment of those children.

Social historians delineate the time from 1700 to 1950 into several eras such as Colonial and Early Federal Period 1700–1830, Period of the Rise of the Common Man 1830–1850, Civil War and Reconstruction 1850–1870; Emergence of Modern America 1870–1900; Emergence of America as a World Power 1900–1920; the Modern Age 1920–   . A study of these periods reveals overlapping of one with another, and a continuity of certain events and trends which extend from one era into the others. Such a temporal quality may be credited to the broad sweep of trends in child care and rearing. A survey of the changing status of the American child reveals that from the Colonial period of the 1700's to the present day, three major epochs stand out clearly. The first of these may be said to have extended into the 1830's, and may be designated as the era of Calvinistic religiosity; the second from the 1830's to the 1890's may be called the period of industrialization, while the last from 1890 to the present time (a period contemporary to many of us) is one to which a variety of names may be applied—atomic, age of the World Wars and the great depression, age of despair and of the destruction of mankind—but for the purpose of our discussion may be marked out as the time of the greatest humanitarian advance.

Let us now examine more closely the first of these eras, 1700–1830. It was a theological age. Religion dominated the child's education, recreation and hygienic care quite as much as his manners and morals. Children were reminded of the fact that their stay on earth would be short, as it well might be. Although families were large, often numbering twenty-five children, there was a high mortality of children and their mothers. The history of the clergyman Cotton Mather was typical; of sixteen children only one outlived him, nine died in infancy, one before the third birthday and the rest before reaching the third decade. Children of the American colonists were constantly admonished to spend time preparing for life-after-death, and to remember the wages of sin and the rewards of virtue. This was a time when fears were realistically abundant, but also when fear as such was used as an instrument for teaching discipline and for enforcing obedience of rule and law. Repression of feelings was encouraged, especially those considered to be evidence of human frailty, such as envy, anger, hatred and feelings of sex. Children were to be seen but not heard; they were tolerated as passive members in a group of adults; in fact they were considered men and women in miniature. There was a clear line drawn between the roles of the male and female, with strong preference for the former who by inheritance and training occupied a super-ordinate position in the family and in the affairs of the community.

Books for children in this early Colonial period were purely theological in content. The Bible was most popular, for religious education, and for learning to read and write. Other books bore such titles as, *Remember Thy Creator in the Days of Thy Youth; Spiritual Milk for Boston Babies; War with the Devil; The Young Man's Conflict with the Powers of Darkness; The History of Goody Twoshoes, with the Means by Which She Acquired Learning and Wisdom.* Although such stories as, *Jack the*

Giant Killer were known to the early colonists, they were not recommended because they were not purely of a religious or moral nature. Any books which promised entertainment were considered vain and worldly. Children were not thought of as growing and developing persons with a capacity to learn, but rather as ignorant men and women; hence nothing was written especially for childish intellect or interest. Primers, spellers and Catechisms were provided adults and children, without differentiation between the needs of one from the other. Even the text books were flavored with pietism.

Cotton Mather gave the following as the educational aim of his time: "They should Read and Write and Cypher, and be put into some agreeable Calling: not only our Sons but also our Daughters should be taught such things as will afterwards make them useful in their Places. Acquaint them with God and Christ and the Mysteries of Religion, and the Doctrines and Methods of the Great Salvation."

Medical care of children was based largely on folklore and superstition, with much of the treatment carried on by lay persons—old women particularly—who were credited with intuitive understanding of children and their needs, and with skill, because of the fact that they had taken care of many children. Even though many of their patients died in spite of, or even because of, their ministrations, this did not detract from their reputations as healers. In spite of deadly epidemics of smallpox, typhoid fever, malaria and dysentery, there was apathy in matters of public health among lay people, and controversies raged between physicians about the contagiousness or noncontagiousness of disease. This was characteristic of the general indifference of the colonists to the scientific progress which was beginning on the Continent. Seventy-one years after

Harvey described the circulation of the blood, his work was still the basis of questioned debate at Harvard.

Much of the disinterest in medical advance stemmed from the belief that illness was of divine origin, with intent to punish the child and to teach him that suffering made him courageous, humane and better aware of the dangers of life in general. Spiritual values were placed on sickness and suffering. The shocking record of infant mortality was accepted as part of God's work, and the dosing with household remedies was believed Providence inspired.

This is not the place to give a lengthy account of the eating habits of American colonists, but it may be pointed out that even some food symbolized morality. Confections were forbidden, not so much because they "undermined" the health, but because they destroyed the "tone of their minds" and made ungrateful and discontented citizens. Moral reformers said eating of sweets for pleasure paved the way for later evils such as using strong tea, coffee, snuff, tobacco and fermented liquors.

During the middle of the Colonial period, marked by end of War for Independence, a gradual change in the religious and education status of the child developed. The moral and religious standards of the American child were modified, in time becoming milder and permitting more pleasure to come into his life. The philosophy of secular utilitarianism in American life began to be practiced; if good conduct was practiced, it brought temporal advantages as well as rewards after death. Now some books for children cautioned children "to be good," not only to escape the punishment of hell, but also in order to be prepared for a successful life in this world. In them, children were taught that learning to spell paid off in dividends and rewards of material things. Morality paid off in tenfold

87

success. *How to Make Money* was a title of a book for children which summarized the philosophy of Americans who were developing the resources of our country. Even the poorest boy was reminded that he had a chance to become rich, particularly if he was "educated," had a trade, and was morally good and of religious bent.

The development of deism helped to remove the overtones of fear which were associated with so many of the thoughts and acts of the Colonial child and his parents. By 1830, rules of conduct in child rearing followed religious principles less than examples of virtue exemplified in stories of men and women who through honesty, thrift, industry and sobriety achieved "success." Standards of discipline changed, parents becoming increasingly aware of the fact, which today seems common place, that coercion itself is not discipline. Reminiscent of present-day child-rearing practices is the concept expressed in the 1830's that parents should "appeal to reason" in disciplining and molding behavior of their children, and should "spare the rod"—this without danger of spoiling the child.

Although the Colonial education system was originally religiously oriented and to a great extent church-controlled, after the Revolutionary War secularization began, and after 1780 vocational training began to be provided in a limited way within the framework of the school system. This development was not accepted readily by many of the professional educators, but with the growth of towns and cities, better methods of communication, transportation, and industrialization, public education changed also and was modified accordingly.

Values attributed to recreation and to the function of play were modified only slightly from the beginning to the end of the period we are discussing. The early colonists asked that recreation of the young be "lawful, brief and seldom." By 1830, play was permitted for health reasons, being qualified by the age and sex of the child, and being restricted to moderation. However, the area of child care which received least benefit of national progress and growth was that pertaining to physical health. While the medical profession had made advances in studies of disease pathology and in a beginning control of the communicable diseases, there was still abundant ignorance and superstition both within and without the field of medicine.

A beginning was made in public health as cities took over care of the water supply, paved the streets and instituted drainage of houses. The pioneers in this public health movement were laymen who more than the physicians worked for measures of improving community health.

The second great period of American history to be reviewed in this paper extends from the 1830's to 1890. During those years the colonizing process continued to develop new ways of life and new values, but the Americans continued to borrow ideas and philosophies from the Old World, and then to modify them in keeping with their own needs. This is seen particularly in the field of industrialization and in the areas of child rearing and education. In England and on the Continent the great industrial revolution had started. As this influence was felt in America it changed not only the methods of day labor, but habits of family living and child care, education and the conduct of business. It was the forerunner of the age of scientific development.

With the development of the factory system, the labor market increased and many youths at early age went to work outside the family. Children had always been valued assets in the economy of the colonists, and now continued to serve as buffers against financial insecurity. The employment of children in factories caused no shock to the public sentiment because children had always been expected to work. Few people realized the difference between work on the farm or in the home, and in the factory where they often worked sixteen hours a day. Children were exploited because of shortages of labor and their parents were criticized when they counseled adolescents against early marriage. Society had need of children, wanted large families and aided in the early emancipation of child from parent. This was true not only for boys but also for girls, because there was a great need of women not only as the bearers of children but as workers in factory and on farm. The child was part of the economy; in times of labor shortage he was exploited, put to work early; in times of surplus he was kept in school longer, encouraged not to marry and to remain living with the family.

In spite of the need for many children, society did not have the methods of reducing the high mortality of children. Very slowly came a realization of the benefits of conserving the life and health of children. In the field of child rearing, ideas of reformers rose to dominance. Having cause to rebel against what they experienced and witnessed in inhumane treatment of children, and stimulated by the European writers Rousseau and Pestalozzi, American authors increasingly criticized the artificial and excessive restraint imposed on children by adults. As a result, greater freedom was permitted children; they were listened to and attempts were made to treat them more as individuals having a unique status, and as equals instead of as inferiors. They were accorded rights in keeping with their immaturity. Although there still was a great difference of opinion about the proper methods of disciplining children, more and more the wisdom of those who, oddly, were often religious dissenters as well (Quakers and Unitarians) was admitted to be reasonable. The philosophy of moral suasion, appeal to reason and training in resourcefulness and independence grew in acceptance, although opponents of these views then, as now, claimed that it led to indulgence and weakness of the will, and was the cause of impudence in children, as well as of delinquency and national corruption.

The humanitarian movement which was to gain great momentum in the next several decades had its real beginnings in the movement for the abolition of slavery. Influenced by the antislavery movement in Europe, and by the stand taken in this country by the Quakers, efforts of the abolitionists increased not only for the eradication of slavery, but also for the improvement of welfare of Negroes and whites alike. When the Thirteenth Amendment was passed by Congress, reformers were free to turn their attention to such matters as temperance, woman suffrage and care of the unfortunate. Financial panics and the increasing urbanization brought into the foreground problems of poverty, slum living, public health and child labor.

During the winter of 1864–65, New York City had more than two thousand cases of smallpox with 600 deaths; Philadelphia in the first year after the Civil War had over 700 deaths due to typhoid and 334 to typhus. These were followed by years with even greater mortality due to epidemics of these and other communicable diseases. In 1866 New York City established a municipal board of health, and efforts were made to clean up tenement houses and to vaccinate the citizens. However, care of the indigent, prisoners in jails and the mentally sick continued to be deplorable. Children were not differentiated from adults as all were thrown together in overcrowded institutions.

The first organized protection of children was the outgrowth of humane measures improving the care of animals. In 1874 a girl of nine, beaten and starved by her foster mother, was carried into court in New York City as an animal on complaint of the Society for Prevention of Cruelty to Animals because there was no law for the protection of children against cruelty. In that court was organized the New York Society for Prevention of Cruelty to Children. Other organizations aimed at improving the welfare of children were developed; many of them were part of church and religious movements such as the nondenominational Y.M.C.A. Private philanthropists sponsored the establishment of public libraries, schools and colleges. However, social needs continued to outrun social provision in meeting them. This was partly due to the poor management of public institutions set up to care for the needy. An important development in the 1870's was the setting up of social agencies which attempted to bring order and good management to private and public charity organizations. Among the most prominent examples of those dealing with children was the settlement house, Hull House, in Chicago, which started kindergartens, clubs, a day nursery for children of working mothers and a penny-savings book. Welfare workers could not avoid recognizing the fact that the people they dealt with were usually victims of social and economic forces which were inhumane; this led welfare workers, despite ridicule and taunts which labeled them "socialists, anarchists and atheistic meddlers," to support all movements of social uplift such as abolition of child labor, sanitary housing, penal and public health reform and campaigns against municipal corruption.

Throughout the 1890's the people of the United States

of America were imbued with the feeling that although the greatest of centuries was coming to a close, still greater were yet to come. The valuation of "greatest" had different meaning to industrialist, factory worker, public health official, physician, social worker and the humanitarians in general. To the latter, it meant more opportunities to cure the abuses and injustices of society. Life in America had become complex; as Professor Woodrow Wilson observed in a paper entitled, "On Being Human" (1897), "Once it had been easy to be human, but now haste, anxiety, preoccupation, the need to specialize and make machines of ourselves have transformed the once simple world. . . ." As the twentieth century started, a paradox was apparent. Capitalists who were accused of greedy and ruthless exploitation of working men, women and children, lavished millions of dollars on hospitals, libraries, schools, churches and museums. In the words of Andrew Carnegie, "The millionaire was but a trustee of the poor." As panic turned out hordes of unemployed, philanthropic efforts rose and the lot of the common man in general seemed improved by the multitude of new mechanical inventions, through labor-saving within the home and in industry, through improved plumbing and sanitation, fire protection, water and food purification, and public hygiene. More schools were being built in city and country, and a high-school education was a normal expectation. There was a deepening conviction that ethical and humanitarian measures had a vital relationship to economics and that if this kinship was not respected, it might lead to economic disequilibrium.

The third and last period to be discussed in this paper covers the first half of the present century. The last fifty years have condensed time, as Henry James predicted; the past forty years have witnessed terrifying changes. Before the First World War, our people along with all Western civilization, were profoundly optimistic and confident that the progress of the preceding century would continue; only a few historians and novelists foresaw the confusion, violence and death ahead; and few social scientists foresaw what would happen to children.

Although everything that befalls adults also influences the lives of children, only a few of the major forces will be reviewed here as having specifically modified the status of children in the past four decades.

An impression of the economic and social realities of American life at the beginning of the twentieth century may be gained from statistics showing the distribution of wealth. At that time, one per cent of the people owned as much as the remaining 99 per cent owned together, and 80 per cent of the people lived a marginal existence. Wages were low, yet standards of living constantly improved because of the use of machines and large-scale manufacturing which decreased the cost of production. Out of this industrialization the nation's wealth advanced tremendously, and in time this was reflected in higher wages, and in greater expenditures for public schools, roads and sanitation, while the new millionaires contributed to higher education and medical research. Despite the criticism of a few "muckrakers," there was only mild questioning by the people generally of the ethics of a civilization which allowed a few men to accumulate much of the wealth and then dole small portions of it back to charity.

America was filled with contradictions. On the one hand there were unparalleled wealth and natural resources, yet these were unevenly distributed; the lot of women in the home was better because of labor-saving inventions, yet social legislation affecting women lagged behind that of other nations; children fared better as a whole, yet child-labor practices continued to be horribly inhumane; there was a larger leisure class and more individual leisure, yet a large segment of the population worked at least twelve hours daily, six days a week. Chaotic as all this was, it bred a social consciousness which led to the greatest humanitarian movement of all time.

It was natural that the drive for social justice should embrace the rights of children. Interest in the life of children was increased by the practice of birth control, which was beneficial in reducing the stress and strain which often came to all members of families of many members, and which made the individual child more precious to his parents, and therefore an object of more concentrated care and attention. Along with these feelings came greater anxiety to parents who began to doubt their own abilities in child rearing. Young persons approached parenthood with exaggerated apprehension which made child rearing unpleasant for parent and child alike. Minutiae of normal behavior came to be looked upon with concern by mothers who too often were led to believe that they were responsible for so-called "problems," a feeling still too prevalent among mothers today.

It was natural that persons concerned with improving the lot of children should turn for aid to the sciences. Big business in the U.S.A. had learned that scientific research fostered bigger business, and gave industry advantages in competition. Scientific research became a form of business pioneering. The physician, like the farmer, merchant and industrialist, became aware of the usefulness of science in solving problems. Medical research became scientific instead of remaining empirically clinical. As a result, contagious disease began to be attacked with new weapons forged out of the discoveries of Pasteur, Lister and Koch. Out of these attempts to control disease and to reduce infant mortality arose the science of pediatrics. Pediatricians, along with colleagues in the public health movement, have consistently fostered prevention, as well as control and eradication of disease. The success of these efforts is easily measured; in fact one of the scientific advances of this century was the development of more accurate methods for collecting vital statistics pertaining to our national health. From these we learn that infant mortality for the first year of life decreased from 100 per 1000 live births in 1915, to 32 per 1000 live births in 1948; this saving in lives was due to the control of diarrhea and the communicable diseases of the respiratory tract, particularly pneumonia and influenza. Childbearing became safer; public health measures almost wiped out smallpox, typhoid and diphtheria. In more recent years, medical science has been ever more successful in the management of physical disease because of the discovery of the antibiotics and because of biochemical and biophysical approaches to the diagnosis and treatment of physical pathology.

Concurrent with these developments in medicine and public health have come advances in nursing, education and psychology; education and psychology were at first quite apart from medicine, but later these disciplines brought together their theories and knowledge and exchanged ideas and techniques. One example of such an interchange was witnessed in the development of American child psychology. Psychologists and educators, such as G. Stanley Hall, C. L. Thorndike, William James and John Dewey, through their work on learning, first in animal psychology and later in learning of humans basically altered the ideas of child development and set apart child psychology from the rest of psychology. The psychiatrist Adolf Meyer, and the founder of psychoanalysis Sigmund Freud, although representing different philosophies, were in agreement that personality is a summation and synthesis of all aspects of life—biologic, economic, cultural, sociologic and psychologic—and stressed the importance of early childhood in the development of happy adults. As time went on this concept laid the foundation for new teaching in child care for parents as well as for professional workers in medicine, nursing, social work, public health, education, the clergy and the law. Indeed, psychology seemed to be the concern of everybody, and many people turned to it for personal as well as professional guidance. Freudian psychoanalysis aimed at removing some of the taboos regarding human behavior and in de-emphasizing the need for punishment in character development, thus helping to eliminate potent sources of unreasonable fear and guilt which have become recognized as prominent symptoms of the neuroses. Today dynamic psychiatry, just as some religions before it and now, aims at helping individuals solve psychologic conflicts and, more important, emphasizes the importance of providing a happy and healthy childhood in which the capacity to love and to be loved is learned early through experiences with one's parents. Childhood is appreciated as a valuable phase of life in itself, not an ordeal to be speedily passed through in order to attain a more blissful state in adulthood. In the manner of the teachings of Rousseau, the modern parent is encouraged to rear his child in a simple, natural environment in keeping with his special needs and immaturity, so he may have all the advantages of having lived a life of his own. The child is encouraged to have contact with other children whom he is not afraid to challenge, whom he can defy and who can defy him, so that out of these experiences he may become socialized and may develop that sense of reciprocal relationship with his fellows which fosters a self-imposed desire for fair play.

Interest in child psychiatry and its application to medicine, education and child care received impetus from efforts at dealing with juvenile delinquency, which caused so much national sentiment after World War I. Out of this concern developed an active mental hygiene program, and the establishment of the first child guidance clinics. Although national organizations promoting physical hygiene had been established before this (the Child Health Association, for example), now official bodies such as the National Committee for Mental Hygiene, assisted financially by the Commonwealth Fund, effectively fostered progress in helping children who were mentally disturbed and in trouble, or who seemed destined to become emotionally sick. Emphasizing the importance of the teacher and the school in helping children grow emotionally as well as intellectually and socially, the child guidance clinics were more than treatment centers, and for the past thirty years have continued to serve a broad function of work with children, including parental guidance and the training of professional persons in psychiatry, social work, psychology, pediatrics, nursing and public health.

Such a widening of scope and interests as exemplified by the present-day child guidance clinic characterizes the merging of interests and the interdisciplinary character of other child care programs. Today the U.S. Public Health Service is supporting this child psychiatry program in a creative manner and on a national scale.

It would be remiss if mention were not made of the work and influence throughout our country of the Federal

Children's Bureau. Established in 1912, to study problems of child labor and to systematize inquiries into child life, this agency of the government has most effectively stimulated and developed welfare programs of every variety which have become models for other nations, and which may yet prove to be more effective agents for winning international peace than are our most modern weapons of warfare.

The work of the U. S. Children's Bureau has been highlighted each decade since it was set up by a White House Conference. Exemplifying again the interests and trends in child care work, the last Conference emphasized the importance of the whole child, his individual worth and his proper development emotionally and physically, and brought forth recommendations from professional persons in many disciplines, and from parents and youth itself, which are to serve as signposts in the years ahead for all workers with children and those most responsible for their rearing and care. It was recognized that comparatively little is known about the personality development of children, and hence it was concluded that concerted efforts by professional persons in different disciplines should be focused on study of the child in as scientific and objective a manner as possible. As a consequence, there is a renewed interest in the establishment of child study centers at a few American universities where medical science, education, the social sciences and the humanities may combine in a comprehensive program of study and teaching about children and their development and behavior, which will benefit not only professional persons and parents, but which will contribute to the advancement of social progress in our country and in the world.

As an example of the function of such a child study

center I may describe best the work at Yale with which I am associated. The Yale Child Study Center was developed as the central agency in the University for teaching and research dealing with the growth and development of infants and children. Its staff consists of physicians, particularly pediatricians and psychiatrists, psychologists, social workers, educators, psychoanalysts and a sociologist. There is readily available co-operative assistance from other departments in the University representing other fields.

We are particularly concerned with the training of medical and nursing personnel and school teachers, who represent disciplines responsible for most of the professional care of children in our country. We are convinced that if the teacher, with the pediatrician, nurse, social worker and others had a greater understanding of, and feeling for, the principles underlying growth and development, and of the dynamic qualities and interrelatedness of the processes involved, there would result more effective child care and teaching than we now provide. Accordingly, at Yale there have been set up programs for postgraduate training of pediatricians, public health personnel, and educators which have a common focus. Attempts are made to help these students acquire knowledge of the biologic, psychologic and social mechanisms which operate together in a well-ordered and regulated manner, and which result in various behavioral patterns. An important part of the training is received through direct observation of children of all ages, both well and sick, in different settings such as the well-baby clinic, nursery school, elementary school, high school and hospital, where the same children may be observed over a period of time (the longer the better), and where each trainee is provided with supervisors who by experience and knowledge can help the student observe, record, contemplate and understand what is noted. It is hoped that through these supervisors who represent different disciplines, a translation and application of this new knowledge may be made within the framework of child care, whether this be medical care, nursing care or classroom teaching, and that physicians, nurses and teachers will become alerted to the emotional implications of everything they do, and yet coincidentally will become aware of their limitations in dealing with the psychologic aspects of child care and not strive to be amateur psychiatrists.

As an outgrowth of these experiments in teaching graduate students at Yale, have come beginning attempts at modifying the training of medical undergraduates. Without underestimating the need to continue studies of disease by microscope and animal experiments, or by clinical examination, it is our belief that psychologic and sociologic studies of the human being, well and sick, are equally important, and that in medical education this approach must not only be taught to students by formal teaching exercises, but must be demonstrated by precept and example. This is not easy to do, because students and faculty frequently feel uneasy when participating in a break with tradition which emphasizes methods of patient study and care from which results are less tangible than statistics marking a fall in death rate or the recovery from an illness. The trend nevertheless seems to be in the direction of a greater alliance between the humanistic sciences and the medical sciences throughout the training period of the medical student.

A slogan came out of the last White House Conference which had been unspoken and taken for granted for a long time. "As Children Go, So Goes the Nation," is the watchword. Militarists and those concerned with fortifying a nation against warfare have long been aware of the need to protect the young, to conserve their health, and to provide them with the right kind of education. But there are others, the nonmilitarists, who strive for peace, who are equally aware of the need to strengthen youth and help it to develop in a healthy fashion, not because of the older view of economic necessity, but rather for the very purpose of promoting peace and preventing war.

The child came to the serious attention of our society as an object of reform. With the rise of science, attention focused on him as an object for scientific study, first in the realm of his physical self, his intelligence and learning, and then more lately in the sphere of his emotional and social development. Business and industry have long proclaimed, and to a great degree proved, that modern man is master of his economic and physical fate. With more exact knowledge about emotional development and behavior has come a similar belief about the predictability of his future as a feeling, acting, and thinking human being. It has been said that if we could raise a single generation of children who in infancy and childhood had experienced a lessening of repression of the natural tendencies of love, sympathy and co-operation, there would result not only a greater expression of humanitarian endeavor, but a social order at home which might help modify social orders abroad. The difficulty is that at the present time each year seems to bring greater obstacles which interfere with our attempts to give children love and security, out of which they may in turn develop the attributes just enumerated. Many of us are disturbed by the frequent breakdown in family life, by the intolerance of difference in religious beliefs, and maybe most of all, by the witch-hunts aimed at any person who today professes greater desire for peace than for war, and for international good-will than for nationalistic enterprise.

Whether the convictions that many of us hold regarding the importance of children and the plastic nature of their characters, in terms of indoctrination for peaceful, healthy and creative group living are borne out depends on many things. That the child will continue to be considered an object worthy of care and study seems certain. But what the aims for this conservation as well as the products of our efforts will be depends in the last analysis on you and me—the parents and parent surrogates of our nation's most valued resource, our children.

ENVIRONMENT IN NUTRITION

Russell M. Wilder, M. D.

IT IS fortunate that man, more effectively than any other form of life, has been able to adapt to his environment; or, rather, through the exercise of his intelligence, man has learned how to modify his environment to meet his needs. Thus, by use of suitable clothing, shelter, and various mechanical contrivances, he so regulates the temperature of the air around him that he lives, without too great discomfort, either on the arctic tundra or in the jungle of the Amazon. So also, using oxygen, he can climb the highest mountains, or in airplanes ascend to twice the elevation of the highest Himalayan peaks, without untoward effects. By the same exercise of his intelligence, he successfully protects himself against attack by other predatory animals— although less effectively against attack by other men—and from disease-provoking germs and viruses, although less successfully against the viruses. Even so, vaccination against the smallpox virus was one of the early triumphs of immunology.

Man's control of his environment has been especially successful with respect to his supply of food and drink.

Before the dawn of history he had domesticated certain animals and birds; thereby he overcame the uncertainties of hunting to meet his food needs. He next developed agriculture, thus further insuring himself against interruptions of his food supply. He increased his flocks and fields more and more, until today with current technical advantages one man's labor is enough to feed fourteen others, at least in the United States. Requiring water, not only for his own consumption but for his fields and gardens, he has assured his supply since very ancient times by building reservoirs and aqueducts.

More recently a great deal of attention has been paid to the sanitary quality of food and water. So currently as only yesterday, cholera, typhoid fever and other diseases, transmitted by contaminated food or water, caused devastating epidemics in the Western world. A story in this connection is related about Dr. John Snow. In the evening of September 7, 1854, Dr. Snow proposed to the vestrymen of St. James' parish in Golden Square in London that the handle be removed from the Broad Street pump. The vestrymen were dubious. All the residents had filled their pitchers at this pump for centuries. But within ten days 500 people had contracted cholera. So at Dr. Snow's insistence they "stopped the pump's foul flow" and cholera disappeared from Golden Square. This early triumph and many subsequent discoveries at last awoke the public and their legislative representatives to the need for sanitation, and since then state and local boards of health have been given the authority to control the purity of supplies of food and water. The result has been the virtual elimination of waterborne infections in this and other of the more progressive countries of the earth.

The result of application of sanitation has not been

Russell M. Wilder

quite so good with food-borne disease, although here again great progress has been made. It is now recognized by almost everyone that food and food utensils can carry the germs of tuberculosis, brucellosis, scarlet fever, diphtheria and a variety of other diseases, and sanitary programs for control of the handling of food in restaurants and markets meet with general approbation. However, even in the decade closing in 1948, some 3,000 epidemics were traced to milk and other foods. Constant vigilance is called for. Fortunately, the rapidly improving methods of refrigeration help tremendously to prevent the growth in foods of dangerous bacteria; and pasteurization of milk is being practiced widely, although not as widely as desirable. Some 50 per cent of the fluid milk sold today has not been pasteurized, although in five states and in 500 municipalities milk pasteurization is compulsory. The practice should be universal.

NEGATIVE EFFECTS OF FOOD ON HEALTH

The food environment has both positive and negative effects on health. I am coming to the positive effects, namely improvement of health through better diets; but first, on the negative side, in addition to the hazards from imperfect sanitation, I must mention hazards that attend the use of additives to foods. Some such additives are incidental, others are intentional. Lead and arsenic used in spraying fruit trees, D.D.T. and other organic chemicals for control of insects, leave residues on foods which may be poisonous. Those are the incidental additives. Intentional additives include not only certain health-guarding vitamins and minerals, but also mold inhibitors, antioxidants, bactericides, emulsifiers, synthetic flavors, sweeten-

106

ers and artificial coloring. Many of these practices are advantageous; others are deleterious. All of them demand and are receiving the attention of nutritionists and sanitarians.

Contrary to some hysterical statements made mostly by food faddists, no harm of serious consequence is apparent at the moment from the use of additives. This is the conclusion recently announced by the Food Protection Committee of the National Research Council's Food and Nutrition Board.[1] The report of that committee is based on extensive study of the problem and on a review of the evidence presented at the hearings of a Congressional Committee and at other hearings held by the Food and Drug Administration. It had this to say: "Contrary to some ideas that have been circulated, reliable food processors have not reduced the nutritional quality of our foods or created inferior products through the use of chemical additives. . . . Likewise, there is no evidence that consumption of foods resulting from the use of the new materials in crop protection or in the production and processing of foods have created mysterious disease epidemics or endangered the health of the people." The report cited three examples of the use of intentional additives which the Committee regarded as in the interest of the public health. The examples were addition of iodine to table salt as insurance against goiter; fluoridization of drinking water to reduce decay of teeth; and the enrichment of flour and bread with vitamins and minerals, as protection against pellagra, anemia, and other nutritional deficiency diseases.

[1] The National Research Council was inaugurated in 1916 under a congressional charter for the purpose of providing an independent cooperative body of scientific counselors to the Government. The Council is composed of representatives of more than ninety of the major scientific societies of the nation, including representatives of engineering and industry.

Discussing "incidental additives," the report clearly implies that without the use of pesticides not enough food could be grown to feed the people of this country. Danger is recognized, but it can be avoided by adequate scientific study and effective regulation. Formal tolerances for lead, arsenic, fluorine, and D.D.T. are expected in the near future; informal tolerances have been in use for some time. Although the Federal Food and Drug Administration examined many samples of fruits and vegetables in the past year, only three were found to exceed the tolerance for lead arsenate, and none contained a dangerous amount of D.D.T.

The report asserted further that the manufacturers of these chemicals, the U. S. Public Health Service, the Meat Inspection Service, and the Insecticide Division of the U. S. Department of Agriculture, and the Food and Drug Administration are alerted and on guard against the hazards of chemical additives to foods, and that forty of the states now have legislation to regulate the use and sale of such chemicals.

Much more could be related to show that the public, their legislative representatives, and their government's officialdom have been quick to put to work the discoveries coming from research in the realm of sanitation; and also that the hazards from contamination of food and water have largely been diminished. The negative effects of food today are quickly recognized. I cannot say as much, however, for the application of what is known about the positive effects of food; and yet the maintenance of a satisfactory nutritional environment means not only assuring freedom from contaminants, but attention to the positive effects. For on these positive effects of food may depend resistance to disease, the mental alertness of the population, and the vigor of the race.

POSITIVE EFFECTS OF FOOD ON HEALTH

Those who are trained in the sciences underlying nutrition know that the human body requires for growth, maintenance, and productive activity a mixture of foods of good nutritional quality—in other words, a diet which will supply at regular intervals a minimum of thirty or more nutrients. I should like to review what is meant by nutrients in some detail.

We have all heard that foods contain one or more of three classes of foodstuffs—proteins, fats, and carbohydrates. An example of a nearly pure protein is the white of egg; a nearly pure fat is butter; and a highly pure carbohydrate is cornstarch. The foodstuffs, after their digestion, are absorbed into the body. There successive chemical changes reduce them to component parts, with a consequent release of heat and other forms of energy. The energy is measurable in calories. One of the first requisites of a diet is that it supply a sufficient number of calories— not too few, for then weight is lost as the body devours itself to release the energy required for life; and not too many, for in that case all of the food is not degraded to yield energy and the excess is stored as deleterious fat.

I am sure you recall these concepts of the food classes— the proteins, fats, and carbohydrates—but do you know that the several proteins, such as those in meat, beans, cereals and dairy products, differ markedly in composition? Each protein is made up of a variety of amino acids. Not less than eight of these are essential nutrients—essential not only to life, but also in the sense that they cannot be produced within the body and must, therefore, be contained in the diet. I need not bore you with their chemical names—lysine, tryptophan, and so on. The point is that the diet must supply a certain minimum of each essential nutrient to promote growth or to maintain the status quo, and that in general, the animal proteins of meat, eggs, and milk, are superior to the proteins in vegetables from the standpoint of the amino acids they contain.

Your food, that is to say your diet, must provide protein of such a quality that the necessary minimum of each essential amino acid is made available. Furthermore, to be of maximum value they ought to be provided at every meal. Research has shown that the several amino acids must march along together if the tissues are to use them to the best advantage.

With the fats and carbohydrates, you need not be so much concerned as with the proteins. To a large extent fats and carbohydrates are interchangeable. Both are sources of caloric energy and the one can replace the other, except that diets extremely low in fats are usually not particularly appetizing and that some fat is required to enable the body to absorb certain other nutrients, namely those vitamins which are soluble only in fat.

This brings us to the vitamins and minerals. Foods supply not only calories and proteins but a wide variety of vitamins, such as vitamin B_1 or thiamine, B_2 or riboflavin, C or ascorbic acid, vitamin A, vitamin D, and many others. They likewise supply salts of sodium, potassium, calcium, iron, and other minerals.

There is a natural law which the late Professor Lafayette Mendel was first to call the "law of minimum." It is quite as rigid as are other natural laws. This law prescribes a certain minimum allowance for each nutrient. I mentioned before the requirement for a minimum of each essential amino acid. Similarly the law demands a minimum allowance of each of the several vitamins and minerals.

I suppose you are wondering how in the name of Providence anyone who is not an expert in nutrition can plan his eating so as not to make mistakes in so complex a business or how our ancestors, without any formal knowledge of nutrition whatsoever, managed to survive.

The answer is simply that our ancestors didn't do so well, that many of them were not as vigorous and did not live as long as they might have lived with better diets. As Sandburg said in his *Abraham Lincoln, The Prairie Years,* "The wilderness is careless." Furthermore, we are at an even greater disadvantage in some ways than were our forebears. In their day foods were less sophisticated. Their meats, when they got meat, were not, as are some of ours, processed by high temperatures, which affect unfavorably their nutritional value. Their vegetables were mostly fresh. Some of ours come out of cans, and although the canning industry has greatly improved many of its products, some vitamins as well as some amino acids are hurt by processing. The flour used by our grandmothers in baking bread was ground between stones, whereas ours is ground between steel rolls and more complete separations are made of milling products. In consequence, the flour of today is whiter, but lower in natural vitamins. Most important is the fact that our forebears used much smaller amounts of sugar than we do. In one way or another we consume more than 90 pounds per person annually. Sugar supplies calories, but almost nothing else—no amino acids, no vitamins, and no minerals, or at most small traces of these nutrients. The amount of food we eat is determined largely by our capacity for calories, so taking more sugar means taking less of foods containing amino acids, vitamins and minerals. The nutrients of the diet are diluted by the sugar content.

So you see, the nutritional environment has changed in many important ways. In former times, if people got the amount of food they wanted, which wasn't always the case, they usually obtained the nutrients required. Today, however, you can fill up on sweets and fats and products depleted through processing and go short with respect to one or several of the essential nutrients. Many people today, buying only refined salt, develop goiter because the iodine contained formerly in much of the cruder salt of those times is not present in refined salt. Or in using margarine in place of butter, you may run short of vitamin A, unless you make sure that the margarine is fortified with this vitamin which butter naturally supplies.

Well, what can be done to improve this positive aspect of the food environment?

Actually, something *has* been done, but more needs doing. Surgeon General Scheele, not long ago, remarked that the cultural lag between the enunciation of a new idea and public action based upon it has been estimated as thirty years. It is more than thirty years, however, since Marine and Kimball taught us that our diet was short in iodine and that the shortage was responsible for the prevalence of goiter. A minute amount of iodine put in all our table salt would practically eliminate this disease. Salt fortified with iodine—so-called iodized salt—is on the market, but unless you ask for it you may not get it, and you have to know about it to ask for it. Why not require that all salt used for eating purposes be iodized?

I am reliably informed that all our margarine now is fortified with vitamin A. This is a voluntary program of the manufacturers, but would you inhabitants of New York City be content with a voluntary program for the sterilization of your drinking water or the pasteurization of your milk? Why not require fortification of all margarine so that no one would have to question whether it is fortified? In passing such laws, we would only be requiring that essential nutrients be replaced in the diet.

Much of our white flour and a considerable proportion of commercial bakers' bread is labeled with the word "enriched," and when it is so labeled it must contain a certain minimum of the nutrients thiamine, riboflavin, niacin and iron. This flour and bread enrichment program was launched eleven years ago at the instigation of the nutrition scientists of the American Medical Association and the National Research Council. It was not, as has been incorrectly stated here and there, instigated by the millers and bakers. However, for the extensive development of flour and bread enrichment on a voluntary basis, the flour millers of the country and the large commercial bakers were responsible. The benefit to the public health has been significant. Through roller milling of flour and the increased use of sugar, the per head consumption of vitamin B_1 (thiamine) was falling steadily in our country and had reached a dangerously low level by 1940. With enrichment of bread and flour, which involved restoring the more important vitamins, the per head consumption of thiamine was doubled and that of niacin and riboflavin materially increased.

One sometimes hears the comment that enriched bread cannot possibly be equal to whole wheat bread because we do not put back all the nutrients that are lost from wheat during milling. Professor Elvehjem, who is looked upon as foremost among the nutrition scientists of the times, points out that the loss of other vitamins is not nearly as great in milling as the loss of thiamine, riboflavin and niacin, and that these are the vitamins returned to the flour or bread in the process of enrichment. The advantage of enrichment has been widely recognized, and today twenty-six of the states have laws requiring that all white bakers' bread, all family flour, and in several states all corn meal be enriched. The virtual disappearance in this country since 1940 of beriberi and pellagra can be attributed in large part to this program. Beriberi and pellagra are the consequence of severe deficiency of thiamine and niacin respectively. In Bataan, where beriberi took the lives of more than 200 persons every year in a population of only 90,000, the disease virtually disappeared when the white rice, which is the common cereal there, was enriched with thiamine.

Well now, if the need for increasing the consumption of thiamine, riboflavin and niacin is so evident, why are we content to depend on a voluntary program which certainly will break down in time as interest in it wanes? Why not require everywhere, as today is done in many states, that all white flour, all white bread, and all corn meal contain not less than a certain minimum of each of these nutritional essentials? If prevention of the ill effects of poor diets is as important a public health measure as is believed, why not ensure the vitamin and mineral content of every food consumed in quantity? How can it longer be considered reasonable to permit the marketing of foods which fail to carry the nutrients we should find in them? Education of the public in nutrition is helping to secure more widespread use of better diets, but education in nutrition fails to reach many who need it most. Were the nutritive quality of the foods which are consumed in quantity to be assured by regulation, just as is the purity of the water and the milk we drink, the nutritional environment thereby created would make it difficult for anyone to go wrong, instead of as at present requiring special education to go right.

INDEXES OF THE NUTRITIONAL STATUS

The concept that by controlling our environment we may improve the public health is nothing new. The novelty today is that we now possess more knowledge of our relation to our surroundings and have acquired not only more technology but more experience.

The value to the public health of controlling what the people have to eat has been demonstrated convincingly in England since the beginning of World War II. Among the indexes of public health are infant mortality, maternal mortality, and the death rate from tuberculosis. In all other wars, these indexes worsened badly, but in World War II in England they improved. There were fewer infant deaths, fewer women died in childbirth, and the death rate from tuberculosis fell. This occurred despite a serious housing problem, the crowding of people into poorly ventilated bomb shelters, the shortage of physicians, the increased anxieties, and some unavoidable relaxation of sanitary regulations. The only environmental factor unaffected for the worse was the available food, which was improved. With food imports curtailed as they were, the government was obliged to assume responsibility for all food distribution. In consequence, the science of nutrition could be put to work on a gigantic scale. Rationing meant that everyone received his share, and this share for several items—notably milk, meat and eggs—represented more, much more than many people previously could afford to buy. There were also special dispensations for groups with special needs—pregnant women, children, the sick, and persons engaged in very heavy occupations. Also the nutritional quality of all bread was improved, and the margarine was fortified with vitamin A. They did not enrich their flour and bread as we have done. Instead they turned to undermilling their flour. The people did not like its baking quality or coarse gray appearance, but they used it and benefited from it. Undermilled flour molds more easily than highly milled white flour, but this was less of a problem in England than we found it to be here, as the weather there is cool most of the time.

Consequent to this control of the positive aspect of the nutritional environment, maternal mortality, deaths in infancy, and deaths from tuberculosis declined, as I have said; also the health of the people was conspicuously benefited in other ways. This was determined by physical examination of children in schools where similar health surveys had been conducted in prewar years.

Early in 1944 the Government of Newfoundland, aware that many of the people of that island country were suffering from poor diets, decided to demand enrichment of the flour and fortification of the margarine. As a check on the effect of this procedure, a group of physicians was invited to make examinations of a sample of the population in 1944 and again a few years later. The group, of which I was a member, was composed of specialists in nutrition from the United States, Canada and England. Surveys were conducted on the eastern coast of Newfoundland in August 1944, very soon after enrichment of the flour started and again in August 1948. More than 800 persons were examined in each of these years. They represented a fair sample of the population.

The contrast between the condition of the people in 1944 and 1948 was striking. The prevalence of the outward and visible signs of vitamin deficiencies was more than halved. The reddened weepy eyes, the cracked and swollen lips, and the beefy tongues so conspicuous in 1944 had largely disappeared by 1948. Some abnormalities were still as prevalent, but these, notably red, swollen, bleeding gums and tiny bleedings around the hair follicles of the skin, could be attributed to deficiency of Vitamin C, and nothing of significance had been done to increase consumption of Vitamin C. The bread was enriched only with thiamine, riboflavin, niacin, iron and calcium.

Chemical analysis of the blood and urine established beyond doubt that the vitamins added to the flour and margarine had reached the people. The values for thiamine in the urine and for Vitamin A and riboflavin in the blood were very low in 1944, but satisfactory in 1948, whereas the blood values for vitamin C, which could not be added to the flour or margarine, were even lower in 1948 than they were in 1944.

Improvement was noted not only in the more measurable signs of abnormality, but also in the attitudes of the people. They were more alert and more active. This was especially noticeable among the children. Gone to a great extent was their former apathy; they no longer waited patiently for their examinations; and unless they were shooed away, they clustered around the examiners' tables, interested and curious as children ought to be. They swarmed over the decks of our motor boat, "The Christmas Seal," when we docked at outports, and had to be herded off. Also they engaged in games and play, whereas the absence of play had been noted before.

Observations similar to these were made quite independently by another group of nutrition specialists who examined the inhabitants of a village on the western coast of Newfoundland in 1944 and again in 1948; and when at last the health statistics had been compiled for 1948, it was found that those indexes of public health, to which I have referred as showing improvement in England, had improved in Newfoundland. The very high infant mortality had been almost halved; maternal mortality had fallen greatly, as had the death rate from tuberculosis and the general death rate.

Here, in the United States, one finds among the educated classes, which include most of our physicians, a tendency to ignore the importance of nutrition as a problem. We have an abundance of edibles, and, priding ourselves on being the best fed population in the world, we conclude that we are adequately nourished. There are indications that this judgment may be wrong. For instance, the food consumption studies of the Department of Agriculture, which are conducted every few years, although recently showing some improvement, always reveal that a fairly large proportion of the people eat diets that are poor with respect to one or several essential nutrients. Similarly, in New York City, where five nutrition clinics are established, the number of sickly people referred by physicians far exceeds the number that can be adequately treated. Also, here and there the country over, sporadic nutrition surveys involving physical examinations have been made and, with rare exceptions, have revealed an incidence of malnutrition of considerable proportions. Finally, of great concern to many was the extraordinarily high incidence of rejects for military service in World War II. That poor nutrition was in part responsible is scarcely to be doubted.

However, in our country we have had no systematic periodic examinations of the people to tell us whether their nutritional status has improved or worsened in the past ten years; and ten years from now, if our efforts to assess nutritional health are no more systematic than they have been, we shall continue in our ignorance. As a part of any program undertaken to improve the nutritional environment, a periodic health survey ought to be included. A satisfactory program would involve annual or more frequent physical examinations of a scientifically selected sample of the population, the examinations to be made by physicians who have been trained to recognize evidence of nutritional ill health. The program also should include research activities to improve methods for diagnosing malnutrition.

The responsibility for such activities rests squarely on our public health authorities. They, however, for lack of budgetary funds, must move slowly until the public and their legislative representatives come to understand that the positive effects of the food environment are just as important to the public health as the negative effects.

SUMMARY

I have emphasized that man, through the exercise of his intelligence, has modified his nutritional environment to meet his needs. Without this, life today for most of us would be impossible. Of great importance recently, as I pointed out, has been the insistence by the public on control, through sanitation, of food and water-borne diseases. By this means the negative or deleterious effects of food have been minimized. On the positive side, however, progress has been slow. The public and their legislative representatives have not become aroused to the extent to which resistance to disease, mental alertness and the vigor of the race are dependent on the quality of the diet. So the food environment still leaves much to be desired, with resulting ill effects on public health. Education is proceeding and is very helpful, but nutrition education fails to reach many of those who need it most. The nutritive quality of those foods which are consumed in quantity by everyone could be assured by regulation, just as is the purity of milk and drinking water; and with such regulation the nutritional environment could be adjusted so that it would be difficult for anyone to go wrong, instead of requiring, as at present, education and constant attention to go right. As a part of any program undertaken to improve the nutritional environment, a periodic health survey ought to be included. A satisfactory program would involve annual or more frequent physical examinations of a scientifically selected sample of the population, the examinations to be made by physicians who have been trained to recognize evidence of nutritional ill health. The program also should include research activities to improve methods for diagnosing malnutrition. The importance of attention to the positive aspects of the food environment cannot be overemphasized, especially at times like these, when every ounce of manpower is demanded to face calmly and effectively the current threats to peace and progress.

INDEX

INDEX

Académie Française, 71
Additives
    incidental, 108
    intentional, 106-107
    see also Flour, Food, Vitamins,
        Water
Agriculture, Dept. of, 118
Alexander, Leo, 4, 70
American Medical Association, 113
Americans
    at beginning of 20th century, 94
    philosophy of, 88
Ames, Edward Scribner, 29
Anemia, 74
Animals, 51
    mummified, 75
    without brains, 32, 43
    see also Deer, Dogs, Mice, Sheep
Amino acids, 109-112
Anrep, G. V., 51-53
Antibiotics, 96
    see also Penicillin
Aristotle, 28, 35
Art, 26, 44
Artists, 40
Atomic age, 84
Attitudes, rational versus doctri-
        naire, 27

Baal, 21
Babies
    anencephalic, 75
    in relation to mothers, 13
    Mongoloid, 77-79
    premature, 11
    statistics on, 14
    see also Children, Mothers
Behavior
    neurotic, 46-68
    patterns of, 36
    repetitive, 67
    sexually aggressive, 58-59
    stimulus-bound, 56
Beliefs, in relation to reason, 26

Beriberi, 114
Biology of ethics, 20-45
Birth control, 95
Birth rate, study of, 14
Blood analysis, 117
Board of Health, 91, 105
Brain, 32-33, 43
Bread, enrichment of, 113, 116-117

Calcium, 117
Calories, see Diet
Calvinistic religiosity, 84
Carbohydrate, 109-110
Carnegie, Andrew, 93
Case, Shirley Jackson, 21, 27, 29
Cerebrum, see Brain
Chaos, ethical, 40
Charcot, M. J., 35
Child care
    changing concepts of, 83-103
    programs in, 98-101
    trends in, 84, 89, 91-92, 95, 97,
        101
Child guidance clinics, 98-99
Child Health Association, 98
Child labor, 90-92, 95, 99
Child study centers, 99-100
Children
    books for, 85-86
    changing status of, 84, 94
    crippled, 76
    education of, 84-86, 88
    effects of diet on, 116-117
    employment of, 90
    high mortality of, 90
    growth of, 33
    illness of, 15
    in jails, 91
    malformations in, 71-72, 75, 78-81
    medical care of, 86, 101
    Society for Prevention of Cruelty
        to, 92
    see also Babies, Child labor,
        Mongoloid, Mothers

Index

Cholera, 105
Christianity, 27-28, *see also* Religion
Cleft palate, 76, 79-80
Clinics, 118, *see also* Child guidance
Cockroaches, 20
Coleridge, S. T., 23
College of Physicians and Surgeons, 51
Colonial Period, 85-88
Commonwealth Fund, 98
Community
  medical services in, 15
  studies of, 13, 17
  culture of, 18
Congressional Committee, 107
"Copers," 16
Culture, 17, 19
Cyclopia, 76

da Vinci, Leonardo, 35
Darling, F. Fraser, 54, 62, 69
Darwin, Charles, 47, 68-69, 71
Darwinian theory, 4
Deer, 54-56, 62, 69
Defects, congenital, 81-82
  see also Malformations
Deism, 88
Dewey, John, 96
Diet, 109, 112, 114, 116, 118, 120
  see also Nutrition
Diphtheria, 96, 106
Discipline, 24, 88
  see also Fear
Disease
  and babies, 13-14
  control of, 96, 119
  in its local setting, 3-19
  and mental health, 46
  in perspective, 15, 35
  resistance to, 109
  see also Epidemics
Dobzhansky, Prof., 82
Dog (s)
  Darwin's, 47, 69
  experimental, 56, 61
  Pavlov's, 52-54
Drives, 42
Dysentery, 86

England, public health in, 115
Eagle, Solomon, 38
Eclipse, 61
Elvehjem, Prof., 113
Environment
  adverse, 82
  controlling, 114
  and heredity, 70-82
  in nutrition, 104-120
  see also Medicine
Epidemics, 86, 91, 105-106
Epidemiology, 79, 81
Esthetics, 44
Ethics
  biology of, 20-45
  of civilization, 94
  definition of, 21, 35
  foundations of, 36-37
  terms of, 22, 54
  values of, 33
Evolution, 40-41, 43

Family, 95
  spread of disease within, 15
Faun, *see* Mongoloid
Fear and discipline, 85, 88
Federal Children's Bureau, 98-99
Federal Food and Drug Administration, 107-108
Flour, 111, 114-117
Fluoridization, 107
Food
  during war, 119
  "enriched," 113
  negative effects of, 106
  positive effects of, 109-115
  see also Nutrition
Food and Drug Administration, *see* Federal Food and Drug Administration
Food Protection Committee, 107
Fouchet, 24
Freaks, 71, 75, 81
  see also Malformations
French, Thomas M., 67, 69
Freud, Sigmund, 58-59, 68-69, 97

Gantt, W. Horsley, 52

Gene, 71-72, 80
Genetics, 70-74, 81-82
Geneticists, 78
  Mendelian, 70
Gerard, R. W., 20-45
Germ plasm, 77
German measles, 74
Germany, 37-38
Glands, 78
Goats, *see* Sheep
God, 34-35, 38
Goiter, 112
Gordon, John, 81
Government
  in control of disease, 6, 8, 99, 107
  see also Nazi, Soviet
Greeks, 28
Gregg, 74

Hall, G. Stanley, 96
Harvard, 87
  School of Public Health, 79
Harvey, W., 87
Health
  effects of food on, 106-109
  formula for, 40
  statistics on, 118
  surveys, 116, 118, 120
  see also Public Health
Hebridean Islands, 17
Hemophilia, 74
Heredity and environment, 70-82
History, natural, of neurotic be-
    havior, 46-68
Hogben, Lancelot, 73
Holt, L. E., Sr., 9
Hospitals, 10-12
Hull House, 92
Humanitarian movement, 91, 95
Humanity, facets of, 30
Hunger, 50
Huxley, Thomas, 27, 38, 46
Hygiene, 98

Id, 58
Industrial Revolution, 84, 89-90
Infant mortality, 9-10, 115-116, 118
  see also Babies

Influences, environmental, 70
Ingalls, Theodore H., 70-82
Inhibition, 60
Injuries, environmental, 80
Insects, 42, 72, 81
  see also Cockroaches
Intolerance, 102
Iodine, 107, 112

Jackson Memorial Laboratories, 80
James, Henry, 93
James, W. T., 63, 69
Jehova, 21
Jukes and the Kallikaks, The, 73
Jurisprudence, 44

Kant, 38
Kids, 65-66
  see also Sheep
Kimball, O., 112
Koch, R., 78, 96
Kruse, H. R., 46, 69

Laboratory reflex, 52
Lamarck, 71
Lambs, 64-65
  see also Sheep
Laws
  moral, 40
  of obligation, 9
Libido, 42
Liddell, Howard S., 46-69
Life span, 31
Lilly, W. S., 38
Lister, J., 96
Living standards, 94
Locusts, 21
Luther, Martin, 27
Lysenko [Lyssenkow], 70

Machinery, 3
  see also Industrial era
Macrocosm, 71
Malaria, 86
Malformations, 71-72, 75, 78-81
Malnutrition, 118-120
Man, 4, 43-44, 104-105
  natural history of, 47

Index

Marine, D., 112
Maternal capacity, 16
  see also Mothers
Mather, Cotton, 85-86
Maze, 48-50, 53-54, 56, 68
Meat, 111
  see also Diet
Medical profession, 6-7
Medicine
  developments in, 96
  environmental, 5, 17
  in England, 6-8
  preventive, 9
  social, 5
Mendel, Lafayette, 71, 110
Mental health, 46, 69
  see also National Institute of
    Mental Health
Metronome, 54, 57
Meyer, Adolf, 97
Mice, 79-81
Microcosm, 71
Milk, pasteurization of, 106, 113
Minerals, 110-112, 114
Mongol in Our Midst, The, 73
Mongoloid, 76-77
  see also Babies
Mongolism, 79
Monsters, 71, 75-76, 81
  see also Malformations
Motherhood, technique of, 19
Mothers
  adaptation to child, 12-13
  mortality of, 85, 115-116, 118
  of Mongoloid babies, 77-78
  nursing, 43
  pregnant, 116
  see also Maternal
Mouth habits, 64
Murray, Father John, 27

Napier, John, 21
National Committee for Mental
  Hygiene, 98
National Institute of Mental Health,
  59
National Research Council, 107, 113

Natural history of neurotic be-
  havior, 46-68
Natural selection, theory of, 71
Nature, 3-5, 46
Nazi government, 70
Negative feedback, 32
Nervous system, 42
Neurosis, 46, 59-60
  experimental, 52-54
  symptoms of, 97
Neurotic behavior
  natural history of, 46-68
New York City
  Board of Health established in,
    91
  Society for Prevention of Cruelty
    to Children in, 92
  preventive medicine in, 9
Newfoundland, 116, 118
Newman, J. H., 27
Newton, Isaac, 27
Niacin, 114, 117
"Non-copers," 16
Nutrition
  and environment, 104-120
  science of, 109, 114-115
  surveys in, 118
  see also Diet and Food

Org, development of, 41
Oxford University Press, 19
Oxygen, 79-80, 104

Panics, financial, 91, 93
Pasteur, Louis, 96
Pavlov, I. P., 51-53, 68-69
Pediatrics, 8-12, 18-19, 83, 96, 98
Pellagra, 114
Penicillin, 31, 40
Pestalozzi, J. H., 90
Pestilences, 3
  see also Epidemics
Philosophy, 29, 38, 45, 89
Philosophers, 28-29
Physiology, 12, 32
Plato, 11, 35
Protein, 109
  see also Diet

Psychiatry, 83, 97-98
Psychoanalysis, 69, 97
Psychology, 98
    child, 96-97
Public Health, 83, 89, 92, 96, 107, 115, 119, 120
Pump, 105
Purpose, notion of, 31-32, 91

Quakers, 91

Racial supremacy, 81
Ram, 57-59
    see also Sheep
Rationing, 115
Reason, 23, 26-28
Reflexes, 34, 51-52, 57
Religion, 22, 25, 30, 37, 39, 84, 86, 88
Research, 28, 95
Reymert, M. L., 69
Rh factor, 72, 74, 82
Riboflavin, 114, 117
Rosenberg, 71
Rousseau, J. J., 90, 97
Russia, *see* Soviet Russia
Ryle, John, 19

St. Hilaire, Geoffroy, 75
Salt, 112
Sandburg, Carl, 111-112
Sanitation, 105, 119
Scheele, Surgeon General, 112
Science, 33-34, 36-38, 44-45, 95
    definition of, 22-25
    criticism of, 31, 38
    physical, 38, 46
    values in, 22, 24, 30
    versus religion, 29-30
Scotland, experiments in, 54-55
Self-love, 42
Senn, Milton J. E., 83-103
Shakespeare, 26
Sheep, 48-54, 56-66
Slavery, 91
Smallpox, 86, 91, 96, 104
Snow, John, 105
Social agencies, established, 92

Social justice, 95
Social science, 46
Social medicine, *see* Medicine
Social work, 98
Society, abuses of, 93
Society for Prevention of Cruelty to Animals, *see* Animals
Society for the Prevention of Cruelty to Children, *see* Children
Solar system, 41
Soviet Russia, 71
Spence, Sir James, 3-19
Startle-stimulus, 53, 57-58, 60, 64-66
"still reaction," 62-63
Stress, 79, 81
Sugar, 111-112
Sunburn, 73-74
Superiority, innate, 70
Superstition, dogmas of, 40
Syphilis, 75

Teeth-grinding, 64-65
Teleology, 31
Theology, 29, 38
Thiamine, 114, 117
Thirteenth Amendment, 91
Thorndike, C. L., 96
Thyroid gland, 51
Truths, universal, 34
Tuberculosis, 15, 106, 115, 118
Twins, 76
    Siamese, 75
    see also Lambs
Tyndall, John, 37
Typhoid, 86, 91, 96

Unitarians, 91
United States
    big business in, 95
    historical periods in, 83-84
United States Public Health Service, 108
United States Children's Bureau, 99
Universe
    regularity in, 23
    scientific view of, 39

Index

University of Chicago, 29
Universities, 4, 6-7

Values, 32
  absolute, 34
  religious, 29
Van der Horst, L., 67, 69
Veedor counters, 60
Vegetables, 111
Virchow, Rudolf, 78
Virtues, Graeco-Christian, 30
Vital statistics, 96
Vitamins, 110-117

War, 4
  see also World War
Water, 105, 107, 113

Wealth, effect on nation, 94
Welfare, 92
White House Conference, 99-101
Whooping cough, 15
Wilder, Russell M., 104-120
Wilson, Woodrow, 93-94
Women, 115
  see also Mothers
World War
  I, 31, 84, 94
  II, 115

X-rays, 31

Young, care of, 42-43
  see also Animals, Babies, Children, Sheep